This book is a special gift for

_____

Presented by

_____

Presented on

_____

50 THINGS

EVERY CHILD
NEEDS TO KNOW BEFORE
LEAVING HOME

Raising Children to Godly Adults

DR. JOSH & JEN
MULVIHILL

RenewaNation

Table of
CONTENTS

SECTION 3

A NOTE TO YOUR CHILD
FROM JOSH AND JEN

You may not realize it right now, but this is probably going to become one of your favorite books. Do you know why? It's a book that was written just for you!

You probably know that your parent(s) love you a lot, but have you ever thought about all of the time, energy, effort, and prayers that they invested so that you would grow up to become a mature man or woman who knows, loves, and serves Jesus Christ? Raising a child to become a mature, godly adult who follows Christ takes a lot of work, and this book is a glimpse into the things your parent(s) did on your behalf throughout your life.

This book is a place for your parent(s) to tell you about the spiritual milestones and memories they prioritized in your life and how you arrived at the place you are today. Your parent(s) did their best to apply Proverbs 22:6 to raising you: "Train up a child in the way he [or she] should go; even when he [or she] is old he [or she] will not depart from it."

We hope you will treasure this book. So, if it seems like an odd gift now, hold onto it, talk to your parent(s) about it, ask for more information about the details in the book, and one day you will be happy that you did! You may find yourself returning to this book as your own parenting guidebook, if God blesses you with a child. But for now, enjoy reading the special notes from your parent(s), rejoice in the life milestones as you remember the events of your childhood, and abound in thanksgiving to God for His graciousness in transforming your heart and in giving you a parent(s) committed to raising you in the discipline and instruction of the Lord.

INTRODUCTION

Welcome to *50 Things Every Child Needs to Learn Before Leaving Home.* We wrote this book to help you raise your child to become a mature adult who knows, loves, and serves Jesus Christ. It's a guidebook and keepsake all in one, designed to help you establish a plan and be proactive for each season of your parenting journey. It is also formatted so that you can record your progress, capture special milestones and memories, and give the book as a special gift to your son or daughter. This book will be helpful for new parents who want a parenting plan as well as for parents of teenagers who are thinking about what they need to do to launch a child into adulthood. It's never too early or too late to think about these things. Whether you have eighteen years or one year before your child leaves home, whether you are a married couple or a single parent, this book will prove helpful for you.

So, grab a cup of coffee, find a cozy chair, and enjoy! Here are a few suggestions to help you get the most out of this book:

How to Use This Book

1. To begin, we suggest that you read the book from beginning to end so you have a strong foundation and a big-picture vision for what we are trying to accomplish. After that, come and go as you wish—use the book as a planning tool to prompt ideas on a do-it-yourself parenting retreat, as a guide to

chart your parenting path, and as a journal to mark milestones and preserve memories.

2. **Think of this as a guidebook,** providing helpful directions and advice from individuals who have been where you are going. A guidebook is full of useful information and important milestones, and it is customizable based on one's preferred path. A guidebook is different from a cookbook. Cookbooks provide exact ingredients in a detailed formula. The cook's job is to follow the recipe. Parenting doesn't work this way. Children are not like apple pie. Parents are not guaranteed a specific result if we put in the right ingredients or if we avoid the wrong ones. Yet that is exactly what many Christian authors recommend. Many parents have absorbed an unbiblical approach to parenting based on behaviorism, resulting in the belief that if they do X + Y they will get Z. That's not what we are advocating. God provides parenting principles in the Bible, and we are helping you apply those to everyday life. We created this book to point you in the right direction, not to dictate every detail. This book takes a holistic look at parenting and addresses the most critical areas we should focus on to raise a child to become a godly adult.

3. **Utilize the book as a planning tool.** It's a planner because it's meant to be interactive—created for you to write in and to make your own. You can add your thoughts, ideas, and preferences throughout the book. You will also find that you can record parenting accomplishments and activities. In the past, a logbook was a place for sailors to keep track of how far they traveled, and that's exactly what you're doing—keeping track of where and how far you've traveled as a parent. So mark it up and use it to plan, track, and celebrate! In section 3, you will find a blueprint for a Do-It-Yourself Parenting Retreat, with self-guided questions to help you plan.

4. **We designed this book to be a keepsake** and hope you will give it to your child as a gift in the future. We created the book so that you can record

milestones and memories, which will be meaningful for your child when they get older, especially if they become a parent. This book may function as a guide for them, just as it did for you.

5. After reading the book, consider a day or weekend on the calendar and schedule a Do-It-Yourself Parenting Retreat to begin planning. Utilize the suggestions and guided questions in the back of the book as well as the chart on page 62 and 63 to identify key parenting priorities for each child for the next six to twelve months. Repeat this process each year so that you are working on one or two of the items in this book at a time with each child. If you commit to do this year after year, you will be amazed at how much you can teach your child over time.

6. Work hard to develop a strong relationship with your child and capture their heart. A wise parent with grown, godly adult children told Jen and me, "Sadly, I know of far too many parents who have lost their children's hearts at young ages, which led to rebellion." No parent I know aims for a conflict-filled or emotionally distant relationship with a child, but if you find yourself in this place, then it is wise to do what you can to strengthen the relationship today. It is beyond the scope of this book to discuss how to develop and maintain a strong parent-child relationship, so our purpose in mentioning this here is to raise awareness that the state of the parent-child relationship impacts how a child will receive instruction and to encourage you to prioritize your relationship at every age and stage of your child's life.

The book is broken down into three sections. Section 1 addresses the importance of having a parenting plan, provides examples of unbiblical plans, and explores what Psalm 127 says about parenting. Section 2 provides fifty things every child needs to learn before leaving home. You will find a brief explanation, some ideas and tips, and places to record your preferences and progress. Section 3 provides you with a Do-It-Yourself Parenting

Retreat including instructions and guided questions to help you plan and assess as well as a milestones and memories section so that you can capture some important events and personalize this book for your child.

A Breakfast to Remember

When I was seventeen years old my parents invited me to join them for breakfast at a local restaurant. Eating out was a special occasion for our family, so I wasn't sure if I was in trouble or being rewarded for something I had done. Turns out, it had nothing to do with my actions and everything to do with my parents' plans.

After we sat down for breakfast, my parents slid a single piece of paper across the table for me to look at and my dad said, "Josh, in nine months you are leaving for college. We want to make sure we have done everything we can to prepare you for adulthood." "We want to know," added my mom, "Is there anything on this list that you think has not been accomplished in your life?"

I had never seen that piece of paper before, but when I looked at it, my childhood and teenage years flashed before my eyes. The paper contained approximately fifty bulleted items, and next to each was a checkmark and a date. As I looked at the list, I remembered when my parents taught me how to honor God by managing money through the creation of savings, giving, and spending accounts. I recalled the many weeks that my parents taught table manners, how to properly address an adult with respect, and how to shake a hand. I remembered when my dad taught me to develop strong academic study skills. I recalled being taught how to pray and read the Bible by my parents.

My parents had spent my childhood and teenage years systematically working through the items on that list and had invited me to breakfast to evaluate with them so they could put the finishing touches on years of intentional parenting. They had accomplished most of what they set out to do, but I remember one particular item on that piece of paper that I told them they hadn't taught me: small engine repair. Why my parents included that on the list, I will never know. They probably recognized a weakness in me and decided to focus energy in this area. I told them that small engine repair was a lost cause. To my relief, they crossed it off the list. And to this day, I hire a mechanic if I need work done on my engines. Aside from small engine repair, I gave my parents the green light for everything on the list.

I share this story because I hope my parents' example encourages you to think seriously about preparing your children for adulthood. Far too few parents have a biblical vision for parenting and far fewer have a plan to implement it, which leads to all kinds of potential problems, missed opportunities, and decreased effectiveness as parents. Not only do we want to help you avoid that, but we want to help you raise children who are passionate about Jesus, who love God's Word and live according to it, and who become mature adults spiritually, emotionally, intellectually, socially, and financially.

Your Roommate Will Thank Me

I remember my first day at Bible college. My parents drove me to my dorm room, helped me unload, and with tearful hugs blessed me, then headed home. And with that, I was officially launched into adulthood. I remember sitting in my dorm room feeling a strange mix of excitement about the new freedom but some trepidation as well. Part of my apprehension was due to the reality that I had two roommates I had never before met or spoken with, and knew nothing about but would now live with for the next eight months. Our time together became a quick lesson in how parents raised their children. My roommate Trevor became one of my best friends. I quickly learned that he was a hard worker, sharp thinker, smart financially, and fun to be around. Together, we experienced an eight-month adventure with our other roommate, Chris.

One day when I came into our room, Chris's bed was gone. It hadn't been removed but was buried under a pile of clothes and other random objects, including dirty dishes and garbage. Chris rarely picked up after himself. When he was finished with something, he would simply toss it on his bed, and over time the pile grew so large that it fully covered his bed. At night he would simply burrow himself under the pile, which worked out okay due to cold Minnesota winter nights. If we'd had separate rooms, it may have been more tolerable, but we all shared one big room, and Chris's messiness impacted us.

At the end of the year, we had to deep clean our room before leaving for the summer. Chris left much of his mess for Trevor and me to clean, so we got bottles of bleach and set to work. I remember one item vividly. It still makes me shudder when I think about it. As we were filling bags with garbage, I picked up a plastic zip-lock bag that was full of liquid. It was watery with a greenish tint, and there were chunks of mold on some small shriveled pieces of whatever was left of the item. Upon further inspection, we guessed it was a decomposed cucumber that had likely sat in that bag, somewhere in the pile, for months.

My mom used to tell me, when I was growing up and complained about picking up my room or doing chores around the house, that my future roommate or wife would thank her one day. I would laugh when she said that because I thought it was silly. Turns out she was right. There are a lot of things our children need to learn to help them mature into responsible, respectful, and well-rounded individuals who love Jesus and live for Him. This book will help you achieve that outcome.

A Long and Difficult Road to Adulthood

My experience with Chris wasn't an outlier or an isolated case. In our generation, a quiet crisis has taken place for young people that has teenagers arriving at the doorstep of adulthood who are not prepared to launch well. This situation is so common that it is known as emerging adulthood. Did you know that adolescence now stretches into the mid thirties? That means individuals are still learning how to be adults into their thirties. Our culture lives in perpetual adolescence: a search for identity that is always becoming, but never mature.

> A quiet crisis has taken place for young people that has teenagers arriving at the doorstep of adulthood who are not prepared to launch well. This situation is so common that it is known as emerging adulthood.

The road to adulthood is a long one for many today. Most of the young people who leave home at eighteen will not marry, become parents, or find a long-term job until they are at least in their mid to late twenties. Many young people in their twenties are not making the transitions historically associated with milestones of adulthood such as marriage, career, parenthood, and home ownership. Postponing commitment, freedom from responsibility, uncertainty, and anxiety are characteristics common to the young adult years. Young people are not assuming the weight of adult responsibilities until much later than they have in previous generations. In fact, a new phrase was created to describe the experiences of this stage of life: adulting. Many young people do not believe they have reached adulthood.

There has been a change in the cultural view regarding the meaning, purpose, and method of becoming an adult. Previous generations were eager for adulthood, but today's generation sees the obligations associated with adulthood in a different way. For a growing number of young people, marriage is to be avoided, children are a burden, and a mortgage is often undesirable. Previous generations saw marriage and parenthood as achievements, but more and more young people see them as problems to avoid. Marriage, parenting, and a career mean the end of independence, opportunity, and freedom. Unprecedented freedom, prolonged college education, the shattering of moral norms, and a lack of accountability create an environment that encourages immature adulthood. Society grants people in their twenties a long delay and does not expect them to take on adult responsibilities but rather allows them to gradually do so at their own pace. The twenties have become a period of preparation and self-definition, or a time of indulgence and unfocused energy. It is an interlude for many rather than a season to take seriously. There are many factors that have affected the road to adulthood.

Four Factors that Make for a Difficult Road to Adulthood

 Identity Exploration. Young people are encouraged to explore and embrace their true self in areas of gender, sexuality, and work. They are trying to understand who they are and what they want in life, searching for a tribe to belong to, a cause worth believing in, and a vision for the person they want to become. They are asking, "Who am I?" Confusion, self-definition, and a desire for clarity mark this season of life.

 Uncertain Future. The young adult years are transient ones, with moves from college to back home with parents or to an apartment, and getting established in a career. If society is unstable morally, economically, or politically, it discourages risk taking. The early adult years are often filled with pain, turmoil, and trauma rather than happy moments and memories. As a result, failure to launch and boomerang adults who return to live at home are common.

 Unlimited Options. Activities and experiences during the child and teen years are part of the process that shapes identity formation in a young person. A variety of opportunities during the teen years helps a young person learn what they enjoy and are good at. Young people are asked to prematurely answer the questions "What kind of work am I good at?" and "What career would I find satisfying for the long term?" Working at home or part-time will help a young person learn their abilities and interests and can be a training ground for the skills needed for adulthood. In addition, decision-making is new for young adults. What to have for dinner? When to clean? How late should I stay out? Where should I live? Should I go to church? Decision-making is difficult for many young adults, especially when the wisdom of Scripture is not guiding life choices.

 License for Irresponsibility. When the watchful eyes of parents are removed and there are no more household standards to follow, what will keep a young person from becoming a "girl gone wild" or the wayward son? We have given young people a license for irresponsibility and no clear role in society other than setting styles and being consumers. Teen bashing is common. Teenagers are regularly treated as incompetent people who cannot control their impulses or hormones. Today's young people serve a sentence of presumed immaturity regardless of their attitudes or actions. Often, children and teens are treated as something less than real people. A pastor I know calls teenagers "pre-people." The belief that a teenager is an unfinished person gave rise to the juvenile justice system. They are expected to rebel, engage in risky behaviors, and not conform, and as a result they are not held accountable—to their own detriment. Our culture suggests that young men are to show their prowess not at work but on the sports field. The young woman who is ready to be a mother is told to go to college, start a career, and wait a decade. The culture's perspective on young adults is pessimistic, accountability is limited, and expectations are minimal.

The childhood and teen years are the time when individuals will acquire the good or bad habits they will have the rest of their lives. J.C. Ryle correctly observed the force of habits in life and reminds us why the child and young adult years are so important:

Habits have long roots. Sin, once allowed to nestle in your bosom, will not be turned out at your bidding. Custom becomes second nature, and its chains are threefold cords not easily broken. Well says the prophet, "Can the Ethiopian change his skin, or the leopard his spots? Then may ye also do good, that are accustomed to do evil" (Jer. 13:23). Habits are like stones rolling downhill—the further they roll, the faster and more ungovernable is their course. Habits, like trees, are strengthened by age. A boy may bend an oak, when it is a sapling—a hundred men cannot root it up, when it is a full-grown tree. . . . So it is with habits: the older the stronger—the longer they have held possession, the harder they will be to cast out.[1]

One of the factors that determines the well-being of young people is the presence of parents who are actively engaged in their lives and   have high expectations for them. Young people want a close relationship with their parents and are sensitive to their opinions and actions. The cultural view of preteens and teenagers as a strange, deviant creature to fear plays a role in creating low or no expectations that result in immaturity and irresponsibility.

It is an arduous journey to reach adulthood. Becoming a mature adult is highly ambiguous in our culture. Compared with other societies, ours is short on activities or milestones that mark the arrival of maturity and adulthood. We have ceremonies such as high school graduation, leaving for college, and laws that provide privileges at certain ages. Some milestones of maturity are established in homes such as being left at home alone, piercing ears, mowing the lawn, driving a car, and being old enough to date. The limited rites of passage that recognize arrival at adulthood in our society have been supplemented by rites of passage that many young people pursue on their own, such as drinking alcohol and getting tattoos and body piercings, which visually acknowledge their maturity. Many adults see these actions as signs of immaturity, but in a society that has few rites of passage, this is a way for young people to state their arrival into adulthood.

I know my child has become an adult when:

_____

Because adulthood is difficult to verify, the timing, transition, activities, and meaning attributed to it vary widely from family to family. A young person who has arrived at the threshold of adulthood needs to be invited to join the circle of adults, yet many parents are unsure of when, why, and how to do this; parents also wonder about the priorities and parenting goals they should have along the way. If our priorities are God's priorities and our plans are an implementation of God's plan, then we can have the confidence and conviction to parent well. We want to help you avoid regrets about what you should have done—and panic because of what you didn't do—so you can have peace, confidence, and clarity in parenting your child to a mature adult with lifelong faith in Christ.

When I was a child, I spoke like a child,
I thought like a child, I reasoned like a child.
When I became a man, I gave up childish ways.

1 Corinthians 13:11

CHAPTER 1

A HUGE
RESPONSIBILITY

Like most new parents, we were excited to meet our new child. I was so excited for Jen to have the baby that I tried to "help" her go into labor by encouraging her to run up and down the stairs in our home. The funny thing is, it worked. Later that evening, while we were asleep, I was startled awake by an audible POP and Jen telling me that her water had broken. Ready or not, we were going to be meeting our son very soon.

Six hours later we were holding our first child, amazed by the miracle of life, excited to be parents, and feeling blessed to receive the gift of a child from God. I remember holding Jay and thinking, "This is a huge responsibility! I had better figure out what I'm doing as a parent." Up to this point, I had spent a decade working with other people's children and teenagers, but this was different. The stakes were higher, and the responsibility had been given to Jen and I. We didn't want to fail as parents but we had a lot to learn, and that became obvious almost as soon as we left the hospital and went home.

On day four, we visited the doctor for a well-child checkup for Jay. These appointments are supposed to monitor how a baby is doing, but I think they really are to monitor how new parents are doing. And we weren't doing well. The doctor asked us how we were doing, and we both blurted out, "Not well," accompanied by tears. Jen and I had only had Jay at home for a couple of days and we were both exhausted. Jen struggled with breastfeeding, and Jay wasn't sleeping well because he was hungry. If this was a taste of what was to come as parents, we were in for a rough ride!

The doctor was kind. She encouraged us and offered some much-needed parenting wisdom. We went home to apply our new knowledge, but the results weren't much better. So we did what every wise new parent does: We called mom. My mom drove two hours, and the first thing she did was teach us how to properly swaddle a baby. She was the baby whisperer, because Jay immediately stopped crying. And she gave us a few hours to take a nap. That was one of the most amazing naps of our life.

My mom stayed for a few days and taught us how to put a baby on a schedule, and how to feed and care for a newborn. Within six weeks, Jen had trained Jay to sleep through the night and it felt like a major victory for us! Jen and I wanted to succeed as parents, but despite our desire to be good parents and care for Jay, we still struggled. We needed our doctor's help. We needed my mom's help. We needed the help of our church. All these people provided the wisdom, care, and encouragement to help us learn how to parent a newborn.

> Jen and I wanted to succeed as parents,
> but despite our desire to be good parents and care
> for Jay, we still struggled. We needed help.

I'm guessing Jen and I aren't alone. You may have experienced times when you needed help to figure something out as a parent. I'm sure that you are extremely grateful to those who took the time to listen to the struggles, encourage you, share wisdom, and point you in the right direction. We all need people like that in our life.

But you know where that begins? It begins with us admitting that we don't have it all figured out and that we need others to help us. That's humbling. Sometimes it's embarrassing. But in the end, it is usually fruitful. I've been in full-time ministry for more than twenty years, most of that as a pastor, and as I've counseled couples, I have noticed a few things about parents.

1. **We want to succeed.** We desire to be good parents. So we read books, listen to the latest preacher, and discuss what works with parents we admire,

putting into practice whatever is biblical and makes sense. If I were to ask any parent, "Do you want to be a good parent?" the answer would be yes. If success were determined by desire alone, we would have little to worry about. Nobody wants to be a bad parent. Nobody plans for failure. Yet failure is often the result of a lack of preparation on our part.

2. We believe we are doing a pretty good job as parents. Most parents believe they are doing a good job. And why wouldn't we? Our children dominate our thinking. We are concerned with every aspect of our child's well-being. We want whatever is best for our child and we act accordingly. We invest a great amount of time, energy, and resources into our child. And so we think, "What more can I do?"

> We're comfortable planning for our retirement, setting goals for our company, and even for ourselves, but many of us have never considered setting goals for what our children will become.

3. Many of us lack a biblical, God-honoring plan. We have not crossed paths with many parents who can clearly and concisely tell us the outcomes they hope to achieve in their child's life and the plan to attain positive results. We're comfortable planning for our retirement, setting goals for our company, and even for ourselves, but many of us have never considered setting goals for what our children will become. And the fact is that many people spend more time planning for a vacation than they do for parenting. We may believe that we can get by with a minimum amount of effort and that with the help of others we will succeed. This is faulty thinking and a critical error that will surely catch up to us. We would never build a house without a blueprint. It would be chaos. Inevitably, there would be problems. Yet many parents attempt to raise children without a blueprint. Most would agree that parenting is far more important than vacations or new homes, yet they spend a disproportionate amount of time planning for areas that matter less.

This book is our way of helping you, just as my mom helped us. We would love to walk with you through the different ages and stages, all the joys and pains and the ups and downs of parenting—and this is our way of doing that. Our desire is to help you be intentional and think about the kinds of things your child would benefit from learning from childhood through the teen years. Some of the things in this book may already be priorities of yours. If so, that's great! Let it be an affirmation for you. Some of the things may not be on your radar at all. If so, let that be a prompt to help you in your parenting.

It's pretty easy to get busy parenting and go about our days with no real plan, no strategy, or much thought to what will produce long-term fruit in our children. The idea of planning doesn't get most people out of bed in the morning. For some people, talking about planning is as exciting as a trip to the dentist, eating green beans, and shoveling snow from the driveway. I'm grateful for dentists and I've learned to eat green beans because they are good for me. Planning for our children is similar. It may not be at the top of our to-do list, but it is good for us and it will be good for our children. So before we jump into the really fun stuff of the book—the stuff you probably bought the book for—let's take a moment and think about the value of planning.

CHAPTER 2

THE NEED FOR
A PARENTING PLAN

When I was seventeen, my dad decided to teach me the value of planning by learning to use a map. However, he didn't tell me that's what he was doing. I was sitting in the living room when he approached me, car keys in hand. He handed them to me and said, "Let's go for a drive. You're driving." Confused by this, I asked "Where are we going?" With a grin he said, "Wherever you take us. I just want you to drive."

I got in the car, and away we went. I drove for thirty minutes around the northern suburbs of the Twin Cities. I didn't have a destination in mind; I just drove. At first, I drove on highways and roads that were familiar to me, but slowly this changed, and I was directionless as I turned here and there. After a while, I had no idea where I was, no clue what we were doing in the car, and no plan for where I was going.

When my dad was satisfied that we were far enough from home, he told to me to pull over and park. He handed me a map and said my job was to figure out where we were and drive us back home using the map. I tried to find my bearings but was completely disoriented. Even though I had an end destination in mind, I could not identify where I was or find a landmark to help me navigate the way home. I drove and drove, hoping to see a sign that would help me determine my location, but the more I drove, the more disoriented I became.

After driving for a long time, I pulled over, frustrated because I couldn't figure out where I was; I got out, walked around to the passenger side, handed my dad the keys, and said, "If you want to get home, you're going to drive us."

My dad drove us home that day, and the experience provided me with a couple valuable lessons. I learned that I'm directionally challenged and need to rely on others to navigate. Today, I'm thankful for GPS and a wife who has an innate sense of direction. I also learned that it pays to plan carefully where I'm going and have a plan to get there. Knowing the destination and having a roadmap at the beginning would have made all the difference.

> I also learned that it pays to plan carefully where I'm going and have a plan to get there. Knowing the destination and having a roadmap at the beginning would have made all the difference.

When it comes to parenting, many of us are driving somewhere—just as I was as a teenager with my dad—but we lack clarity and a plan. We won't arrive at a desired parenting destination without clarity about where we are going and a plan for how we are going to get there. Every once in a while, it pays to stop and figure out where we are, where we need to go, and whether we are on track or have gotten off course.

The Art of Planning

Planning includes thinking about a set of desired outcomes and the activities necessary to achieve them. Planning helps us to be more intentional parents. A simple definition of intentionality is action by design. It helps us to avoid missed opportunities and to seize the moments. Having a plan actually provides flexibility, because if we know what we are aiming to accomplish, we can keep our eyes open as we go through our day. The discipline of planning is highly recommended in the Bible. Proverbs 14:22 (NIV) says, "Those who plan what is good find love and faithfulness." Planning would have helped me when I was driving with my dad and it will help us be intentional, strategic, and consistent in our efforts to raise children who know, love, and serve Jesus.

> The discipline of planning is highly recommended in the Bible. Proverbs 14:22 (NIV) says, "Those who plan what is good find love and faithfulness."

Ultimately, we plan to get better results. It has been proven that individuals who have goals and keep these goals in front of themselves are more likely to succeed than those who do not. We have heard all the arguments against planning. "It kills spontaneity." "It doesn't leave room for the Holy Spirit." "It isn't biblical." "I'm not a planner, so why try?" Whatever the argument, we hope to convince you that there is great benefit to planning. And that it is biblical. Most would agree, parenting by the seat of our pants isn't ideal.

Six Benefits of Planning

Benefit #1 – Planning Helps Us Take Ownership of Our Child's Spiritual Growth

Planning helps us assume our God-given role as spiritual leaders in the life of our child. As parents, we don't want to abdicate our role to others, which is a temptation for many. Planning builds confidence, clarifies objectives, and gives step-by-step directions so we can seize moments as they arise. Planning helps us increase our potency as parents and achieve greater results in our child's life. Our impact is stronger and felt longer when we plan.

Benefit #2 – Planning Is Good Stewardship

If you were given ten million dollars, I'm guessing you would be ecstatic. You might even feel unworthy to possess such a large sum. If Jen and I were given ten million dollars, we would have no clue how to manage it. We would need to study how to invest the money to receive a maximum return and would be smart to contact professional financial planners to gain wisdom and guidance. If we wished to see this money grow, we would need to act intentionally. Jen and I would be foolish to do nothing with it and hope that it would magically multiply itself and that everything would work out in the end. The Bible reminds us that children are a gift from God, given to us on loan by God for the purpose of cultivating a life devoted to glorifying Jesus Christ and treasuring Him. Just as planning helps us maximize the return of our money, in the same way it helps us to be good stewards of our children.

> The Bible reminds us that children are a gift from God, given to us on loan by God for the purpose of cultivating a life devoted to glorifying Jesus Christ and treasuring Him.

Benefit #3 – Planning Saves Time and Energy

If we were going on a cross-country trip it would be highly inefficient to pull over every thirty to sixty minutes to figure out the next stage of our journey. We would save ourselves a lot of time and headache by planning our course in advance. Parenting is easier with a plan. Jen and I have plans for family meals, holidays, traditions, discipline—every area of life that we can anticipate. Jen and I spend time together every year planning so that the other 350 days go much more smoothly. Because we have a plan, we don't need to set aside time daily or weekly to discuss big-picture parenting matters. We have more time and energy to devote to the actual task of parenting.

Benefit #4 – Planning Focuses Our Efforts

Parenting is a giant task, arguably one of the most important responsibilities we will have in our life. When it comes to raising a child, we have one shot. We need to make it count and we do that by focusing our efforts on the most important areas. Confucius once said, "He who chases two rabbits catches neither." We must determine which rabbits are worth chasing and which we should let go. When we consider all that we need to teach our children, it can be overwhelming. Planning will help us prioritize. For example, in the first five years of a child's life we must focus a high percentage of our energy and effort on establishing a strong relationship and making sure our child learns to understand parental authority and obedience. Obedience is foundational to character development, which will be the focus of the elementary years. Once competency has been achieved in one area, we can move on to other areas of desired growth.

> Confucius once said,
> "He who chases two rabbits catches neither."

Benefit #5 – Planning Shows Us Where We Must Grow as Parents

Based on our experience with parents over the years, a high percentage feel inadequate to teach their children about God. A lot of parents feel intimidated when it comes to understanding and explaining the Bible to their children. Many have concluded that they don't measure up and should let someone else do the job.

With proper planning, however, we can adequately prepare ourselves for each new parenting task. For example, if we know we are going to be teaching our child a biblical view of marriage, we can prepare and gather our thoughts. This helps us stay slightly ahead of our child. For some reason, when it comes to parenting, we believe it is acceptable to get by with what we know. But we need to take the same care in training ourselves to be great parents as we do in other important areas of life. Planning ahead makes this possible and can motivate us to learn and grow so we will be effective and successful in raising our children.

If we cannot succeed in raising our children to know and love God, then all other accomplishments lose their significance. Former president Teddy Roosevelt once said, "There are many kinds of successes worth having. It is exceedingly interesting and attractive to be a successful business man, or railroad man, or farmer, or a successful lawyer or doctor, or a writer, or a President, or a ranchman, or the colonel of a fighting regiment, or to kill grizzly bears and lions. But for unflagging interest and enjoyment, a household of children, if things go reasonably well, certainly makes all other forms of success and achievement lose their importance by comparison."[2]

Benefit #6 – Planning Imitates God the Father

We don't want to spiritualize planning, but it's worth recognizing that God is a God who has a plan for creation. We get a sneak peak into God's plan with every prophecy in the Old Testament. In the New Testament we learn that Jesus will return again to fulfill

"There are many kinds of successes worth having. It is exceedingly interesting and attractive to be a successful business man, or railroad man, or farmer, or a successful lawyer or doctor, or a writer, or a President, or a ranchman, or the colonel of a fighting regiment, or to kill grizzly bears and lions. But for unflagging interest and enjoyment, a household of children, if things go reasonably well, certainly makes all other forms of success and achievement lose their importance by comparison."

Teddy Roosevelt

God's predetermined plan, and the book of Revelation gives us a glimpse into how God's plan will unfold. When Jesus became human, it was in accordance with God's plan for the redemption of mankind.

A central doctrine for Christianity tells us that God did not create the world and then step back and watch His plan unfold passively. He established His plan, made it known in the Scriptures, and is actively involved in seeing His plan become reality. God has desired results in that He wants to be obeyed, enjoyed, and glorified by all. God is a sovereign God who ordains and establishes His plan for eternity. The prophet Jeremiah reminded the exiled nation of Israel that God's plan was not thwarted, "For I know the plans I have for you, declares the Lord, plans to prosper you and not to harm you, plans to give you hope and a future" (Jer. 29:11 NIV). Ephesians 1:9 (NIV) tells us about God's plan, "And he made known to us the mystery of his will according to his good pleasure, which he purposed in Christ." It is important to point out that the plan God has for us centers on Jesus. The plan we have for our children should be centered on Christ as well. We need to be parents of the cross and of Christ. As parents, our plan for our children should be based on the eternal, Christ-centered, God-exalting, disciple-making plan of God the Father for His children.

Planning helps us to align our plan with God's plans, which is pretty important because the Bible tells us that ungodly plans will be frustrated and ultimately fail. When trying to silence the disciples, even Gamaliel recognized that "if this plan or this undertaking is of man, it will fail" (Acts 5:38). The good news is that God's plans will come to pass. Here are some reassuring words from Isaiah 14:24 (NIV), "The Lord Almighty has sworn, 'Surely, as I have planned, so it will be, and as I have purposed, so it will stand.'" There is nothing in this world that can frustrate the plans of God. Isaiah 14:27 (NIV) reminds us of this: "For the Lord Almighty has purposed, and who can thwart him?" These verses should bring us comfort and motivate us to make sure we are implementing God's plan to raise our children in the instruction and discipline of the Lord. These verses should also cause us to assess what is most important to us and what we are striving for as a parent.

Walking in the Dark

Have you ever woken up in the middle of the night, gotten out of bed, and tried walking around in the dark? It isn't easy or enjoyable. Our walk is slow and our arms are in front of us, groping for anything that can provide direction. We have an idea where we are going but are unsure of the location of furniture and doors. The path we must take is hidden. That would all change if we could simply turn on a light. Psalm 119:105 says, "Your word is a lamp to my feet and a light to my path." God's Word is the light we need for our planning. We no longer have to grope around in darkness. When the Word of God is in our mind and heart, it is a guide that leads us on paths of righteousness.

God has a wonderful promise for us: "If any of you lacks wisdom, let him ask God, who gives generously to all without reproach, and it will be given him" (Jas. 1:5). We invite you to take God up on that offer. Parenting doesn't need to be a big black hole of unknowns. God graciously provides clear guidance for us in the Bible, and we want to encourage you to make sure you have clarity on God's principles and priorities for parenting before you jump into the 50 Things. We created a short, simple Bible study you can find in chapter 17 that is titled "Parenting Goals." Read through these passages in your quiet time or during a weekend getaway. They will be the light you need to guide your way as a parent.

If any of you lacks wisdom, let him ask God, who gives generously to all without reproach, and it will be given him.

James 1:5

The heart of man plans his way, but the Lord establishes his steps.

Proverbs 16:9

CHAPTER 3

WHAT IS PARENTING SUCCESS?

Imagine the day your child leaves home and launches into the world. Who do you hope your child has become, and what do you hope he or she accomplishes in life? As you consider the day you launch your child into adulthood, read the testimony of John Paton leaving home, and the godly impact his parents had on who he became and what he valued in life. Paton recalls the day he departed home for the school where he studied to become a missionary,

> My dear father walked with me for the first six miles of the way. His counsels and tears and heavenly conversation on that parting journey are fresh in my heart as if it had been but yesterday; and tears are on my cheeks as freely now as then, whenever memory steals me away to the scene. For the last half-mile or so we walked on together in almost unbroken silence,—my father, as was often his custom, carrying hat in hand. . . . His lips kept moving in silent prayers for me; and his tears fell fast when our eyes met each other in looks for which all speech was vain!

We halted on reaching the appointed parting place; he grasped my hand firmly for a minute in silence, and then solemnly and affectionately said: 'God bless you, son! Your father's God prosper you, and keep you from all evil!'

Unable to say more, his lips kept moving in silent prayer; in tears we embraced, and parted. I ran off as fast as I could; and, when about to turn a corner in the road where he would lose sight of me, I looked back and saw him still standing with head uncovered where I left him—gazing after me. Waving my hat in adieu, I was around the corner in an instant. But my heart was too full and sore to carry me further, so I darted into the side of the road and wept for a time. Then, rising up cautiously, I climbed the dyke to see if he yet stood where I had left him; and just at that moment I caught a glimpse of him climbing the dyke and looking out for me! He did not see me, and after he had gazed eagerly in my direction for a while he got down, set his face towards home, and began to return—his head still uncovered, and his heart, I felt sure, still rising in prayers for me. I watched through blinding tears, till his form faded from my gaze; and then hastening on my way, vowed deeply and oft, by the help of God, to live and act so as never to grieve or dishonour such a father and mother as He had given me. The appearance of my father, when we parted—his advice, prayers, and tears—the road, the dyke, the climbing up on it and then walking away, head uncovered—have often, often, all through life, risen vividly before my mind, and do so now while I am writing, as if it had been but an hour ago. In my earlier years particularly, when exposed to many temptations, his parting form rose before me as that of a guardian Angel. It is no Pharisaism, but deep gratitude, which makes me here testify that the memory of that scene not only helped, by God's grace, to keep me pure from prevailing sins, but also stimulated me in all my studies, that I might not fall short of his hopes, and in all my Christian duties, that I might faithfully follow his shining example.[3]

Oh the power of Christ-centered parents who raise their children to know, love, and serve God! Every parent has some vision of what they see their child becoming, just as John Paton's father had for him, and this vision guides the decisions they make.

Parenting Success

When it comes to parenting, how are we to measure success? A high-achieving child academically? Sports star? Physically beautiful? Popular? Makes it into a prestigious university? Happy? Makes a lot of money? Avoids major mistakes in the teen and young adult years? Prays a prayer for salvation? What exactly is parenting success? And how are we to measure failure in parenting? Our child gets arrested? Wayward child? Ends up living out of our basement? Doesn't go to college? Works in a low-paying job? Becomes an alcoholic or addicted to drugs? A fractured relationship between parent and child? What exactly is parenting failure?

Those are challenging questions, not easily answered. We tend to equate success with high achievement and failure with low achievement. But if we pay attention to Scripture, we can see that it is possible to succeed in the wrong things. "What does it profit a man," Jesus asked, "if he *succeeds* in gaining the whole world but *fails* to keep his own soul?" (Mark 8:36). Let's apply this to parenting and ask, "What does it profit a parent if a child succeeds in gaining the whole world but fails to keep his own soul?"

> "What does it profit a parent if a child succeeds in gaining the whole world but fails to keep his own soul?"

The man who decided to build bigger barns right before he died, was he successful? If we measure success based on money, prestige, and possessions, he was a big success. But Jesus mentions a different kind of success, that of being "rich toward God" (Luke 12:21) and being faithful with little things (Luke 16:10). Then there were the prophets who were outcasts and the disciples who were martyrs. They had few earthly possessions and were disliked by many people. What were they, successes or failures?

What is to be a Christian parent's greatest aspiration? What is your greatest aspiration for your child? When you think about your child's future, does your picture of success look more like that of the man who built a big barn or of the disciples who followed Jesus at great cost? The world tries to convince us that success is things like wealth, happiness, pleasure, popularity, and comfort. The Bible gives us a much different picture of success centered around faith in Christ, obedience, stewardship, and Christlike character. Sometimes, the world's vision for success seeps into our parenting priorities without our recognizing it, and we begin to pursue priorities that take us away from the things the Bible priorities for the Christian life. Take a moment to examine seven common priorities parents have for their child that fall short of biblical aims for parents.

1. Living a Healthy, Happy Life

The desire that children live a happy, healthy life hits at the very core of a parent's heart. The problem is that it isn't enough. In fact, it isn't even biblical. But it is difficult to say no when a daughter looks at you with puppy-dog eyes and requests an item she wants or when your son begs you to sign him up for an activity because it will be fun. What's the harm in saying yes? We want the best for our children, don't we? Don't we want our children to have every opportunity, every good thing, and a better upbringing than we had? Christian parents, out of an abundance of love for a child, are often guilty of being child-pleasing and indulgent. Our motive is love, but our actions do a disservice by catering to a child's many desires. Our motive may be love, but the question is whether it is a misplaced love of a wrong priority. We are told to love God with all our heart, so a parent must be mindful what it is they love—God or some other love that has crept in, pushing God to a place of second love. Parents are not blessing their children by providing them everything they want. Indulgence produces selfishness and greed in our children, not godly virtues. What our children need most is the Good News more than good gifts. Of course, they aren't mutually exclusive, but they do compete for a parent's allegiance.

Instead of seeking happiness from possessions or experiences, Jesus invites us to follow Him by forfeiting things normally sought in human life. This is apparent when He says, "Take up your cross and follow me" (Matt. 16:24) and "sell what you possess, give to the poor . . . and come, follow me." (Matt. 19:21). A willingness to forfeit all, to sacrifice, and to suffer is at the heart of the Gospel. When we follow Jesus, we discover the truth of John 10:10: "I came that they may have life and have it abundantly."

When our children delight in God, they will discover true joy. Happiness is a by-product of following and obeying God. If we seek happiness for happiness's sake, it will elude us. The writer of Ecclesiastes points this out when he says, "To the man who pleases him, God gives wisdom, knowledge, and happiness" (Ecc. 2:26). A happy life will be discovered by those who teach their children to love God and love others. Let us "seek first the kingdom of God and His righteousness, and all these things will be added to you" (Matt. 6:33).

"If we seek happiness for happiness's sake, it will elude us."

2. Raising a Well-Behaved, Moral Child

Behaviorism is one of the biggest problems in Christian parenting. Behaviorism focuses on external methods to bring about internal transformation, and it will either result in raising a Pharisee who delights in his own righteousness or a rebel who could not measure up to standards on his own. We have an incorrect focus when we prioritize behavioral goals apart from the Gospel. We must seek to understand the attitudes and motives of a child's heart and hold out the beauty of the Gospel for a child to embrace. A parent can force or manipulate outward compliance for a time, but without heart transformation, once the child is no longer under our watchful eye, the child's behavior will be revealed as a masquerading virtue that erupts as vice.

Take a moment and consider how you get your child to behave. What methods do you use? When your lovely child is rambunctious and bouncing off the wall, what do you do to get him to settle down? When your child is mad because she doesn't want to wear certain clothes or go to bed or be told what to do—and ends up stomping her feet in anger and slamming the door—what do you do? What discipline methods do you habitually use? Are you a yeller? Do you use bribery? Do you withhold interaction or affection? Give the silent treatment? Groundings or time-outs? Do you focus on the behavior and try to manage it, or do you pay attention to the affections of the heart driving attitudes and actions and focus your attention there?

Biblically, all behavioral problems go back to the foundational problem of sin (Ps. 51:5; Mark 7:21). Parents who want well-behaved, moral children need to focus on the heart. Our child's behaviors are the result of heart corruption—indwelling sin that manifests itself as pride and selfishness. Although children can have physical problems, the primary diagnosis is simple and straightforward. Temper tantrums, arguing, resistance to parental instruction, failure to obey, complaining, and angry outbursts are the result of sin. We must properly understand the attitude of the heart that has resulted in wrong behavior so we can address a child's behavior correctly.

3. Receiving a Good Education

Success for many parents is seeing their child excel in school, get good grades, and eventually go to a good college. We are told to build our child's academic résumé toward that end. For the child this translates into long hours of homework, hard courses to boost GPA, and extracurricular activities to enhance the résumé. In the end, we are encouraged to believe that it is education that opens the door of opportunity in life. While this may be true, the Bible reminds us that the wisdom of the world is foolishness to God. Education is a great gift from a good God, but the ultimate purpose of education is key. What do we want education to accomplish in our child's life? When we are more passionate about our child's education leading to financial prosperity or career prominence rather than their spiritual growth, we know we are missing the mark in God's kingdom.

Biblically, education is discipleship. Its purpose is to shape a child into Christlike maturity, help a child to think biblically, to prepare a child to live wisely in all areas of life, and bend back a broken world to God's original design. The word *education* never appears in the Bible, but the Bible has plenty to say about education using terms such as *knowledge*, *teach*, *learn*, *instruct*, *think*, *wisdom*, and *mind*. The biblical vision for education is centered on and saturated with God's Word, God's laws, God's work, God's character, the fear of God, and godly living. Practically speaking, many parents are educating a child in a way that does not equip them with a biblical worldview, so there are competing values in the child's life and a lack of alignment with godly living. Education exists to help a child treasure Christ and to equip the child for every good work in service to God. Our children can be "educated" and still not understand the ways of God or follow Him. To gain Harvard and lose heaven is not a fair trade. Let us remember the words of Christ, "What does it profit a man to gain the world and forfeit his soul?" (Mark 8:36). If we are going to push our children to excel in something, it should be that they become a man or woman after God's heart, and the best education helps a child to accomplish this goal.

"To gain Harvard and lose heaven is not a fair trade."

4. Being a Productive Citizen

When we held each of our children for the first time, we wondered what these little people would become and what mark they would place on the world. Like other parents, we want to raise children who love their country, bless their community, and are good citizens. However, when we look to the Bible, we do not see this as the primary purpose of parenting. In fact, our children are growing up at a time when the world's idea of being a good citizen and being a good Christian are increasingly not the same thing. Parents who raise children to know, love, and serve Jesus will raise productive citizens. When we do this, we raise a future employee who is hardworking and trustworthy; a citizen who obeys laws and governing authority; a patient, kind, and caring future spouse who provides a stable home to raise children; and a neighbor who is joyful, giving, and gentle. These outcomes are the result of raising children to love God and love others.

5. Just Make It to Adulthood

Some parents have a defensive mindset: They are hoping their child doesn't get pregnant, stays away from the wrong people, and won't get caught up in drugs or alcohol. Caution, prudent decision-making, and admonition to avoid evil are important elements of parenting. However, if we live in fear that our children may go off the deep end and make life-altering bad decisions, it will result in one of two extremes—a permissive parenting approach that allows too much freedom with the hope that big errors are avoided, or a rigid approach that isolates children from the world. Neither is good. The "just make it through" attitude is a passive mindset that sets a parent up more for failure than for than success.

The parent in Proverbs encourages his son to avoid the path of the fool that leads to damage and destruction, but he docs so by presenting a more beautiful and blessed alternative that is centered on trusting in the Lord (Prov. 3:4–5). When children savor the beauty of Christ as more satisfying than anything this world has to offer, the allure of sin is weakened. When children treasure Christ, the alternatives are seen as an ugly replacement. Sin withers when the Gospel is brought to bear on it. Thomas Chalmers states, "There is not one personal transformation in which the heart is left without an object of ultimate beauty and joy. The heart's desire for one particular object can be conquered, but its desire to have some object is unconquerable. . . . The only way to dispossess the old heart of an object of affection is by the expulsive power of a new one.[4]

Sin can only be conquered when Jesus is savored as more beautiful and satisfying than the sin. If our children love and follow Christ, they are less likely to make life choices that do not align with God's Word, which is harmful to themselves as well as the name of Christ.

6. Developing Special Skills

I love sports. I'm a big Vikings and Twins fan. I enjoy watching my children play sports. Jen is a classically trained musician and music teacher and has been teaching children to play music for decades. Athletics, the arts, and extracurricular activities are gifts from God and immensely valuable. They are part of our family life. They also have the potential to dominate the family calendar and even become a household god. When any activity controls us and we order our life around it or have a difficult time saying no to it, then we have given it a place of worship in our life that is only to belong to God.

For many Christians, activities have taken over more of our life, crowding out church attendance, personal devotions, and family meals. All too often parents are telling pastors, "We'll be gone next weekend for the basketball tournament," or "We won't be there because of the dance recital." Parents believe this is acceptable so that children become well-rounded, have life experiences, develop character, and discover strengths. We try to convince ourselves that all the positives outweigh the negatives.

Parents are encouraged to believe that if they don't provide these opportunities for their child then they are stunting their growth and depriving them of important life experiences. When we "need" to do these things, they become something far greater than they were meant to be in our life. When we give priority to activities, we teach our children that

"There is not one personal transformation in which the heart is left without an object of ultimate beauty and joy. The heart's desire for one particular object can be conquered, but its desire to have some object is unconquerable. . . . The only way to dispossess the old heart of an object of affection is by the expulsive power of a new one."

Thomas Chalmers

devotion to sports or the arts is more important than devotion to God and family. When we prioritize anything that requires us to sacrifice weekly church attendance or regular family meals, we communicate a powerful message about what we value most. In a healthy home, children should be surprised they are missing church, not that they will be attending it. Many parents want their children to achieve success in sports so badly that they are willing to sacrifice a lot on the altar of sports, which results in rarely saying no to athletic events that interfere with Sunday worship and regular family meals.

Let us remember that a sport or extracurricular activity is a great servant, but a poor master. Paul reminds us that physical activity has value, but that this value is limited. A helpful passage for us as parents has been 1 Timothy 4:7–8, as we have weighed what to say yes to and what to say no to: "Rather train yourself for godliness; for while bodily training is of some value, godliness is of value in every way, as it holds promise for the present life and also for the life to come." Sports have their place, but godliness is even more important because of its eternal value.

Wise parents do not make activities the god of their home. Make the decision beforehand that you will worship weekly with a local church and be involved with a community of believers. Be comfortable saying no and explain to your children that they cannot be involved in everything. Help them understand that there is a greater yes you are committing to. God uses the language of sports in the Bible, so he is not against them unless they steal the affection and devotion that belongs to Him alone.

7. Implementing the Right Parenting Formula

Ultimately, there are two kinds of messages being communicated to parents. There are some whose foundational message is what you need to do and others whose foundational message is what Christ has already done. The first type makes a model out of the author, the second turns our focus to Jesus. The first place the burden for change on methods while the second place the burden for change on Christ's power.

There is no shortage of parenting books that encourage parents to adopt various methods or models, which in turn will result in transformation for their child. Parents are taught that transformation is the result of methods such as a positive reinforcement, relational connection, redirection, focus on potential, and reasoning with a child. The mechanism for transformation is the model, methods, or spiritual practices employed by parents. The common denominator for many of these books is behaviorism. The promise of these books is that you can achieve your desired outcome by doing the right things.

The Bible is clear that what is needed are not novel methods, but a new heart. We must understand our child's behavior in terms of heart motivation and see that change is the result of a child internalizing the Gospel and seeking to live in obedience to God. The Bible convinces us that children have a sin problem, which is systemic. It is part of every aspect of their nature. It infiltrates everything they do. All behavior is linked to attitudes of the heart. A parent's concern is to reveal a child's sin and help him or her understand how it reflects a heart that has strayed.

One way to distinguish biblical parenting from unbiblical parenting is that unbiblical parenting preaches transformation that works from the outside-in through behaviorism, whereas biblical parenting works from the inside-out through the Gospel. I want you to read the example of one family so you avoid their mistake. They raised their child in the instruction of the Lord but implemented a form of behaviorism. The brokenhearted mother recalls what went wrong:

> She memorized Scripture verses in Awana club and learned the books of the Bible, days of creation, and the Ten Commandments by heart. They were beautiful days that passed into gratifying years; and together, we reveled in the joy of learning about our Creator and his creation. . . .
>
> Fast-forward to my daughter's first year at the university. She came home one day and told me she had watched a film in biology class that showed a whale with legs. I laughed. She didn't. Instead, she said these impossible words, "Mom, I don't believe the Bible is true anymore. I'm not a Christian." . . .
>
> This wasn't a grown child who lacked biblical knowledge or apologetic train-ing. . . . My daughter had never been reborn. My confidence had been misplaced. . . . I knew in my head every individual had to repent, believe, and put their trust in Christ personally to be saved. . . . No amount of Latin lessons, Bible memory songs, or classical literature can do saving work.[5]

"My confidence had been misplaced." That is a powerful statement every parent should take to heart. Our hope is not in doing the right things, but in the Gospel of Jesus Christ. Let us not downplay the importance of doctrinal instruction, apologetic training, or Christian education. However, they are not substitutes for the work of God in transforming the heart. We can't "ought" our child to love Christ. We can't guilt or shame a child to treasure Jesus. We can't bribe a child to obey God. We can't love our child to Christ with positive reinforcement. Heart change is the work of the Holy Spirit.

When a teacher of the law asked Jesus what the most important commandment was, Jesus replied by saying, "Love the Lord your God with all your heart and with all your soul and with all your mind and with all your strength. The second is this: 'You shall love your neighbor as yourself.' There is no commandment greater than these" (Mark 12:30–31). If this is the most important thrust of the Scriptures for our lives, then it is safe to say this should be what we aim for with our children. All other plans are secondary to helping our children love God and love others. The family does not exist for itself alone, but for service to God and others.

One day, not too far off, we will have our turn to launch our child, just like John Paton's father at the beginning of the chapter. What are we aiming for on that day? What is success for us as parents? And what kinds of things can we be doing today to work toward that outcome? Having biblical parenting priorities is part of that equation and so is understanding God's mission for your family.

CHAPTER 4

BEGIN WITH THE END IN MIND

Growing up, my mother would always have us work in the garden with her. We would till the garden plot, help her plant seeds, clear weeds, harvest crops, and prepare them for storage or a meal. I'm convinced my mom had other motives for having a garden. I believe she was primarily growing men more than growing food. The garden provided us some food, but more importantly it was a means to teach me important life principles about hard work, enjoying God's creation, and a way to spend time together. Today, Jen and I have a small hobby farm with a garden, bees, chickens, farm cats, and a dog that functions as a way to grow boys into men and girls into women. There are always trees to chainsaw, wood to split, chickens to feed, kittens to tend to, and bees to care for. We enjoy the farm-fresh eggs, sweet honey, and cute kittens. But more important, these activities provide us endless opportunities to cultivate the heart of each child.

Like Farmers

Parents are a lot like farmers. Farmers prepare soil, remove weeds, water, fertilize and go to great lengths to help crops grow. But in the end, farmers are powerless to turn a seed into an ear of corn. A farmer cannot make crops grow. She can create the best possible environment for success, but that is all. God grows crops. He brings rain to feed and sun to nourish. The farmer is dependent upon God for the growth and outcome of his crops.

Parenting is similar to growing crops. We can cultivate the soil of our child's heart and create the best possible environment for growth to occur, but we cannot create growth in our child's life. The Bible reminds us that it is God who convicts, guides, illuminates, transforms, and draws people to himself. This is critical for us to understand as parents. If we put ourselves in the place of God in our child's life, the results will be catastrophic for our children.

Undoubtedly, the most decisive factors in bringing about faith are not our expertise, methods, or core curriculum—though all are important. Ultimately, faith will not take root and grow unless God, in His sovereign mercy, awakens the heart and makes a dead sinner alive to Christ (Eph. 2:1–5). That is why Christian parenting must be undergirded with humble dependence on God, and a relentless calling upon Him in prayer to bring about faith and maturity in our children.

It would also be a mistake to believe that our children will grow to maturity without any effort on our part. God invites us to partner with Him in a divine-human partnership. We play an important role in raising children. God designed the home to be the center of evangelism and discipleship. God has created families as the vehicle to teach and train children about himself. Our action is required.

The Divine-Human Partnership

Colossians 1:28–29 is a great example of the divine-human partnership at work, as well as our goal as parents: "Him we proclaim, warning everyone and teaching everyone with all wisdom, that we may present everyone mature in Christ. For this I toil, struggling with all his energy that he powerfully works within me." Notice that Paul is hard at work toiling for the outcome he desires. Although Paul is laboring intensely, it is God who is working powerfully. It is God's energy that makes Paul's labor valuable.

The key principle for parents is this:
Your child's maturity in Christ is your priority.

The key principle for parents is this: *Your child's maturity in Christ is your priority.* Paul's ultimate goal is to see everyone presented as mature in Christ. The word *everyone* is repeated three times and includes children and teens, which means this passage is applicable to parenting. It isn't enough to see children grow up to be successful, happy, and responsible adults. Of course, that is good, but Paul tells us the ultimate goal is maturity in Christ.

The word *mature* means ripeness of character. Paul closely connects maturity with Jesus. To be mature is to have Christlike character. Biblical maturity is equivalent to growth into the likeness of Jesus, which means we are only as mature as we are like Jesus in certain areas of our life. You can generally measure your children's maturity in Christ using the fruits of the Spirit. Each fruit of the Spirit presents an opportunity for you to help your children grow in spiritual maturity.

> What are you toiling for as a parent? What do you hope to accomplish in the lives of your children?

Paul states, "For this I toil." All parents toil for something. The question is whether or not we are toiling for the right thing. So let me ask you a weighty question. What are you toiling for as a parent? What do you hope to accomplish in the lives of your children? How do you complete the sentence "I want _____ for my children"? First and foremost, God calls you to work hard so your children mature in Christ. Can you say with Paul that your aim is to "present your child mature in Christ. For this I toil?"

Parenting in Dependence on God

Let us not go about our parenting while forgetting about God. Isaiah 17:10–11 (NIV) is a warning for all of us: "You have forgotten God your Savior; you have not remembered the Rock, your fortress. Therefore, though you set out the finest plants and plant imported vines, though on the day you set them out, you make them grow, and on the morning when you plant them, you bring them to bud, yet the harvest will be as nothing."

Every gardener and farmer realizes the principle spoken of in Isaiah 17. They cannot make their crop grow. They cannot make a plant come forth from a seed. All they can do is create an environment where it is likely the plant will grow. They do this by preparing the soil, fertilizing, removing the weeds, and watering regularly.

In this passage, people had gone about their day-to-day business and forgotten about God. God was not invited into the routine activities, such as growing plants, and as a result, God taught them a lesson by not allowing them to reap a harvest. The plants grew, but they did not produce fruit. The farmer wonders why there is no return on his crop.

This is a helpful metaphor for parenting and a reminder not to go about our tasks in a way that forgets God. For a while it may look like we are doing a good job without much dependence upon God. We may see some buds of growth, but in the end the harvest in our child's life is minimal compared with what it would have been had we depended upon God.

OUR FAMILY MISSION STATEMENT

When Jen and I were young parents, we knew it would be helpful for us to gain clarity around what we were trying to accomplish as parents so that daily decisions and parenting priorities could be aligned with these biblical outcomes. We wanted to begin our parenting with the end in mind. We asked Jen's parents to watch our child (we have five now) for the weekend so that we could seek the Lord's guidance. Over the next two days Jen and I studied the Bible, prayed, and discussed the goals of parenting. By the end of the weekend, we had written eight priorities from the Bible for us as parents, which we framed, and they have hung in our living room ever since. We phrased the eight priorities as questions for each of our children to answer.

THE MULVIHILL FAMILY

TREASURING CHRIST | LIVING IN LIGHT OF ETERNITY

When you stand before Jesus, will you be able to say yes to the following questions:

1. Have you placed faith in Jesus alone for salvation? "If you confess with your mouth that Jesus is Lord and believe in your heart that God raised Him from the dead, you will be saved" (Rom. 10:9).

2. Is Jesus the foundation of your life and work? "For no one can lay any foundation other than that which is laid, which is Jesus Christ. Now if anyone builds on the foundation with gold, silver, precious stones, wood, hay or straw— each one's work will become manifest. . . . It will be revealed by fire, and the fire will test what sort of work each one has done" (1 Cor. 3:11–13).

3. Do you live in the fear of the Lord? "How on that day that you stood before the Lord your God at Horeb, the Lord said to me, 'Gather the people to me, that I may let them hear my words, so that they may learn to fear me all the days that they live on the earth, and that they may teach their children so'" (Deut. 4:10). "The fear of the Lord is the beginning of knowledge" (Prov. 1:7).

4. Do you love God and others in word, attitude, and action? "And you shall love the Lord your God with all your heart and with all your soul and with all your mind and with all your strength. The second is this: 'You shall love your neighbor as yourself'" (Mark 12:30–31). "Therefore, as God's chosen people, holy and dearly loved, clothe yourselves with compassion, kindness, humility, gentleness and patience. Bear with each other and forgive one another. . . . Forgive as the Lord forgave you" (Col. 3:12–13 NIV).

5. Do you believe the Bible and follow its teachings? "Watch your life and doctrine closely" (1 Tim. 4:16 NIV). "So then, just as you received Christ Jesus as Lord, continue to live your lives in him, rooted and built up in Him, strengthened in the faith as you were taught, and overflowing with thankfulness" (Col. 2:6–7 NIV).

6. Is the glory of God the purpose of your life? "All things were created by him, and for him" (Col. 1:16 KJV). "So whether you eat or drink or whatever you do, do it all for the glory of God" (1 Cor. 10:31 NIV).

7. Are you maturing into the likeness of Jesus? "Walk in a manner worthy of the calling. . . . be imitators of God" (Eph. 4:1; 5:1). "And we . . . are being transformed into his likeness with an ever increasing glory, which comes from the Lord, who is the Spirit" (2 Cor. 3:18 NIV).

8. Are you fighting sin and striving for holiness? "Put to death what is earthly in you" (Col. 3:5 TLV). "No one born of God makes a practice of sinning" (1 John 3:9).

This simple document helps us orient our daily activity and parenting priorities to those areas that matter most. It reminds us that Jesus Christ is the only lasting foundation for life and parenting. Any foundation other than Jesus Christ is unstable and sure to collapse. The inadequacy of all other foundations, and plans, will be made known in time.

As parents, all of our methods, techniques, and resources should point to the beauty and value of Christ. Loving Christ redefines our life, our passions, our priorities, and our plans. Christ changes everything. All of life and everything we do is to be built around Christ. Our goal is to raise children who treasure Christ, become like Christ, and live for Christ.

A biblical plan helps us capitalize on every moment and every opportunity to point our children to Jesus, to love others, glorify God, and walk in obedience to Him. The whole purpose of planning is to reinforce what we believe is most important, showing our children the beauty and glory of Jesus. No strategy for raising our children to love God will have any long-term impact if the primary goal is not to help our children know, love, and serve Jesus.

> A biblical plan helps us capitalize on every moment and every opportunity to point our children to Jesus, to love others, glorify God, and walk in obedience to Him.

If you have never developed priorities or a mission for your family, doing so is a helpful exercise. There is nothing magical about a family mission statement; it is simply a written, unified articulation of what your family is all about—priorities, values, and goals. It describes what you want to be and do as well as the principles you want to govern your lives. We have designed a series of self-guided questions in the Do-It-Yourself Parenting Retreat at the back of the book under the Parenting Goals section that will help you explore the principles the Bible provides for parents, the priorities you have for your family based on Scripture, and the goals you choose to focus on for each child over the next six to twelve months.

Here are six steps to help you develop a family mission statement based on biblical principles and priorities:

STEP 1

Set aside an evening, day, or weekend. Put a date on the calendar.

STEP 2

Discuss the questions in the Parenting Goals section found in the Do-It-Yourself Parenting Retreat.

STEP 3

Identify specific principles and priorities for your family from the Bible.

STEP 4

Craft a one- to two-page statement using the space available on pages 306-307. It may take the form of a few paragraphs, a handful of questions, a motto, an acrostic using your family name, or some other creative form.

STEP 5

Display your family mission statement. Place it in a prominent place in your home and reference it regularly. Celebrate when a family member honors one of the priorities or principles or accomplishes a goal.

STEP 6

Evaluate periodically. You may find that as your family grows and matures, you need to update or modify your statement.

Use the space below to capture your ideas, goals, and values. Begin to formulate a draft for your family mission statement.

_____

_____

_____

_____

_____

_____

_____

_____

_____

CHAPTER 5

CHILDREN ARE LIKE ARROWS

When I was a teenager, I flew to Ecuador to spend a few weeks with the Waodani tribe deep in the rainforest. Neighboring tribes called them Aucas, which meant "naked savages." The Auca tribe became famous for the martyrdom of Jim Elliot, Nate Saint, and three other missionaries. The deaths of these five men was ultimately what God used to soften the hearts of the people in the tribe and open their eyes to the beauty of the Gospel. My parents made the unconventional decision to let me spend some time halfway across the world with the formerly murderous tribe transformed by the Gospel.

I was invited by the pilot to help co-pilot a small six-seater plane (even though I had never flown before) over the rainforest and into a clearing cut from the jungle near the small tribe. When we landed, the Waodani were waiting for us. They greeted us with smiles, hugs, a warm welcome, and true to their reputation, did not wear much clothing. The hate-filled, angry, murderous ways of their past had been replaced by a joyful, gracious spirit. During my time with the tribe, they took me by dugout canoe to the location where the missionaries were killed and they showed me the grave of Rachel Saint, who stayed with the tribe after her brother was martyred to share the Gospel with them.

One of the more memorable experiences was joining the men of the tribe for a monkey hunt in the rainforest. We carried eight-foot-long blowguns with a small quiver filled with darts that were dipped in a black tar-like poison, and I was told not to poke myself because I might die. We also carried spears, just like the ones used to kill the missionaries, which caused me to think about my own willingness to sacrifice for Christ. We walked among monstrous, towering trees with leaves so big that when it started to rain we would break one off and it covered us as effectively as an umbrella. The monkeys lived in these treetops. When we found a group of monkeys, we lifted our blowguns, took careful aim, and fired. To my surprise, the darts flew straight and far. They hit their mark, the poison quickly did its work, and the monkeys fell to the ground. Later that night, I ate monkey for dinner.

The greatest impact from my time with Kimo, Dayuma, and the rest of the tribe was an opportunity to see a living example of the power of the Gospel to transform lives. This made a deep impression on my young heart. As a teenager, Jim Elliot became one of my heroes. Here was a young man who lived and died for the Lord and that was a worthy example for a young man to follow. Jim recorded a statement in his journal that has stuck with me my whole life "He is no fool who gives what he cannot keep, to gain that which he cannot lose."

This phrase was similar to one my parents would regularly mention, which became a motto for our home growing up. They would encourage us, "Live in light of eternity." I have three younger siblings, and we've all devoted our lives to serving God in full-time ministry in some capacity. I believe my parents would have been just as happy to see us serving Christ as Christian businesspeople, tradesmen, artists, musicians, civic leaders, or any other vocation. All four of us were drawn to a life in service to Christ because it was attractive in our home and the highest of priorities for our parents. Living for Christ wasn't something we did on Sunday. It was our life. It shaped everything, including how we spent our time as a family, what we did for vacations, the cars we drove, what we watched on television, and our priorities and values as a family. Jesus was Lord over all things in our home. What we read about in the Bible matched how my parents tried to raise the family. Like all parents, my mom and dad weren't perfect. But when they messed up, they owned it, and it was obvious that they were living to honor God. That was attractive.

"He is no fool who gives what he cannot keep to gain that which he cannot lose."

Jim Elliot

When I had children of my own, my thoughts turned to Jim Elliot's parents and what they did to raise a son like him. We're given a little glimpse into the parenting of Fred and Clara, Jim's parents, in the book *Jim Elliot: Missionary Martyr*. We learn that Jim's parents prioritized their Christian faith over all else in life, were committed to their local church, and read the Bible regularly. They raised Jim to trust the Lord, be adventurous, and to live for Christ. They raised a remarkable son. Their example is worthy of imitation and a faithful model for parents.

Not everyone is blessed to be raised by parents like mine or like Jim Elliot's. While we may not have a great earthly model to follow, we have a perfect heavenly Father who gives us the guidance we need in Scripture to raise a child. The Bible is filled with parenting wisdom, and one helpful passage is Psalm 127. It teaches us not to parent in self-reliance, but to trust in God who builds our house. How easy it is to anxiously toil, believing we can accomplish our parenting goals in our own power! Psalm 127 warns us against this so that we do not labor in vain. The Psalmist also reminds us of the important theological truth that children are a gift from God, belonging to Him, given to us on loan by God for the purpose of cultivating a life that is devoted to glorifying Jesus Christ and treasuring Him. Children do not belong to us, but we often operate as though we are free to do anything we want with a child. As parents, we are managers given the role of implementing God's principles, priorities, and plan for a child rather than our own.

Like Arrows

The Psalmist calls children arrows in the hand of the warrior parent, "Like arrows in the hand of a warrior are the children of one's youth. Blessed is the man who fills his quiver with them!" (Ps. 127:4–5). This is a surprising way to describe a child, but it is a helpful metaphor when we reflect on the task of parenting. Let us consider the purpose of an arrow. Why does it exist? What is its purpose? In general, arrows exist to be shot in battle. They provide strength and protection. What light does this shed on parenting? The implication is that children are to be raised as a mighty weapon for God's kingdom to do damage to the darkness. Calling children arrows implies a number of things worth pointing out:

Like an arrow, a child must be prepared. The preparation, or crafting, of an arrow is important. A crooked arrow will not fly straight or hit its mark. It must be carefully shaped or it will not be able to serve the purpose for which it exists. In this manner, children are similar to arrows. Children are commanded to obey parents in the Lord, which makes obedience training the foundation of child-rearing so that children will "fly straight." A child begins to learn to obey God's commands by obeying parental authority. In Deuteronomy 6, the Hebrew verb translated "impress" or "teach diligently" means "to sharpen or to point." Deuteronomy 6 provides a glimpse into how parents sharpen the heart of a child and point them to Christ. According to Moses, all of life provides opportunities to shape and straighten, and to write biblical truths on the developing hearts of our children.

 Like an archer, parents need a clear target. An archer doesn't haphazardly shoot an arrow. He or she takes careful aim and has a clear target in view. The same is to be true in our parenting. Getting a child into a good school, arriving at adulthood, or success in life isn't the end goal. These are all good things, but they are not the main target. We must be crystal clear about what we are aiming at so that we do everything we can to hit the intended target. Society tells us that happiness and success are what matters. The Bible reminds us that we are to raise children in the discipline and instruction of the Lord. We are aiming for Christ and shooting for the cross.

 Like an arrow, children must be released. An arrow isn't created to stay in the quiver. Arrows are created to be shot. They are shaped and prepared for that future purpose. The tendency of parents is to hold on to their children too long. The biblical doctrine of leave and cleave recognizes the reality of releasing a child. Parents tend to cleave to their children or children to their parents. We want to shape and prepare the child like an arrow, so he or she can be released into adulthood fully prepared, ready to fly straight, and hit the target God has for this young person.

Before parents ask, "How should I raise this child?" we have to ask, "Why did God give me this child?" If the purpose is to raise the child for God—an arrow to be shaped and released to serve Christ—then this must inform all that we do as parents. Everything we do should prepare them for this exciting adventure! This is what Jim Elliot's parents did so well. They raised Jim for Christ and released him to God to serve as a missionary. Jim hit the target, and the impact of his life has been immeasurable.

Since children belong to God and are to be raised for Him, how should we then parent? We ought to parent with biblical priorities, purpose, and a plan. We ought to fully rely on God in humble dependence, seeking guidance from the Bible and going to God in prayer on behalf of our family. We are to implement God's agenda for the children He has blessed us with, in faithful obedience to His instruction, and release them to His loving care. When we do that, no matter the outcome, we can place our head on the pillow at night and sleep well, for we have done what God has asked of us.

CHAPTER 6

TAKING
BABY STEPS

When Jen and I were young parents we began to study what the Bible instructed us to do and consider how to holistically implement that as parents. We envisioned our children as adults and began to work backward, thinking about all the things we would need to do to help them arrive at that destination. In the process, we made a list of things they should know, skills they need to develop, and the priorities for us as parents. We covered every area we could think of, big and small. We identified books they should read and traits to develop, fine-tuning the list over the course of our parenting. As we began the process, we realized that it was a lot of work, that it was truly a work of God to transform a child's heart, and that it required Jen and I to communicate and be united in our efforts. We developed a weekend getaway to help us determine our plan, evaluate how we were doing, and get it done.

Fifty things may sound like a lot. And it would be if we tried to do it all at once. We've learned to spread it out over time, to pick one thing and focus on that. Our encouragement to you is to just do one thing and be faithful in doing that. If we each did one thing and did it over the course of time, I think we would be amazed at the impact. So what's your one priority for each child in the next six months? Once or twice a year, Jen and I identify the items we are working on with each child. After we have spent a season working on a specific area, we place a checkmark next to it and a date so that we remember what we did and when. Over time, we can forget. And with five children, we mix up what we've done with each child, so it helps to have a written record. And by the last child, lots of parents start to lose steam, so writing things down helps us finish strong with all our children. Some items may have multiple dates next to them as repetition will be needed for some of these items throughout a child's life. We categorized everything into ten areas, with five priorities in each area. This kept things manageable for us and helped us focus on the most important items.

While not every one of these fifty items is a direct command to parents in the Bible, they each contribute to helping a child know, love, and serve Christ as well as grow into a mature adult in all areas of life. We don't want our child to be like the body builder who has huge arm muscles, but skinny legs because he only developed one area of his body. We want holistic discipleship so that our children will be strong in all areas, for growth into mature, godly adults. Remember, think of this as a guidebook not a cookbook and feel free to customize it and make it your own.

If you're feeling overwhelmed, having doubts, or are discouraged for some reason, just remember this: God chose you to parent your child. That wasn't a mistake. He believes you are the right person for the job, and He promises to be your rock, refuge, and help in time of need. With God's help, you've got this! The Bible teaches us that having a healthy fear of the Lord helps us to overcome all other fears in life, including those we have as parents.

One of my favorite movies is *What About Bob?* Bob is paralyzed by his fear of germs, which prevents him from experiencing the richness of relationships and many of the joys of life. Bob is fearful of leaving his apartment, touching doorknobs, and riding on an elevator, so he rarely leaves his home. Bob knows he has a problem, so he seeks help from Dr. Leo Marvin, who teaches him how to take "baby steps" and just do the next thing. That's good advice for all of us. Sometimes we just need to take the next step and then the next step, and before we know it, we've gotten somewhere!

In the movie, Dr. Marvin goes on vacation with his family to his lake home and tells Bob that he won't be available for a month. Bob panics, finds out where Dr. Marvin's lake home is located, and shows up unannounced at his door. Despite Dr. Marvin's pleas for Bob to go away, Dr Marvin's wife and children invite Bob to dinner, and his daughter invites Bob to go sailing. Bob was completely overwhelmed about sailing, but to his credit, he goes. The next scene shows Bob tied by rope to the mast of a sailboat, arms stretched out wide, exclaiming, "I'm sailing. I'm a sailor!" By the end of the movie, Bob is cured of his fear of germs—and it all began with baby steps. While the therapeutic ideas of *What About Bob* won't heal anyone in real life, the concept of baby steps is good advice and is helpful as we think about this book. Don't focus on all 50 Things. Start with one thing, then go to the next.

So, take a look at the list and decide, what's your one thing for each child for the next six months? Then, take baby steps.

50 THINGS AT A GLANCE

Firm Foundation

- ☐ Obeys parents and respects God-ordained authority.
- ☐ Knows and understands the Gospel.
- ☐ Owns a Bible and is familiar with it.
- ☐ Trained to worship God through family worship.
- ☐ Baptized as a public expression of faith.

Christlike Character Development

- ☐ Taught the Fruit of the Spirit.
- ☐ Trained to serve others.
- ☐ Taught to understand suffering.
- ☐ Learned personal responsibility.
- ☐ Gives and receives forgiveness freely.

Biblical Beliefs and Worldview

- ☐ Taught core doctrines of Scripture.
- ☐ Knows the why of beliefs and can defend faith.
- ☐ Developed a biblical worldview.
- ☐ Developed a biblical view of manhood and womanhood.
- ☐ Developed a basic understanding of church history.

Spiritual Growth

- ☐ Knows how to study the Bible and have daily devotions.
- ☐ Knows how to pray.
- ☐ Knows the great hymns of the faith.
- ☐ Memorized key Bible verses.
- ☐ Participates in weekly corporate worship.

Life Skills

- ☐ Knows how to care for a pet.
- ☐ Understands how to navigate the internet and social media.
- ☐ Knows how to communicate well.
- ☐ Developed an appreciation for nature.
- ☐ Knows how to responsibly drive and maintain a car.

Relational Skills

- ❑ Confident in making introductions.
- ❑ Learned how to develop and maintain a friendship.
- ❑ Knows phone, text, and email etiquette.
- ❑ Knows why and whom to date.
- ❑ Prepared for marriage and sex.

Work and Money Management

- ❑ Exhibits a strong work ethic.
- ❑ Developed a biblical view of money.
- ❑ Knows how to create a budget and manage money.
- ❑ Understands the danger of debt.
- ❑ Knows how to manage time wisely.

Home Management

- ❑ Knows how to cook simple meals.
- ❑ Knows how to clean the house and do laundry.
- ❑ Knows how to use common tools and has basic sewing skills.
- ❑ Confident as a host or guest.
- ❑ Knows how to care for the lawn, garden, and outdoors.

Personal Care

- ❑ Taught manners and knows common etiquette.
- ❑ Taught personal hygiene and maintains a good appearance.
- ❑ Knows how to respond in an emergency.
- ❑ Understands nutrition and maintains a healthy diet.
- ❑ Knows how to dress appropriately.

Educational Essentials

- ❑ Taught to read and be a lover of great books.
- ❑ Appreciates music and has musical opportunities.
- ❑ Proficient at basic math.
- ❑ Encouraged to explore artistic opportunities.
- ❑ Learned how to write well.

50 THINGS

EVERY CHILD
NEEDS TO KNOW BEFORE
LEAVING HOME

CHAPTER 7

FIRM FOUNDATION

OBEYS PARENTS AND RESPECTS GOD-ORDAINED AUTHORITY

The Bible instructs children to obey their parents, as unto the Lord, and states that this is the first command with a promise (Eph. 6:1–2). This is of first importance to get right with children. Learning obedience at an early age is foundational to all areas of a child's life. A child who does not obey their parents is a child who will live in a constant state of strife. We have taught our children that obedience should be joyful and immediate. It is to be without complaint, without delay, without excuse, and without argument. Taking the initiative to teach obedience will eliminate power struggles and conflict with your children down the road, and will point them toward holy obedience to our Lord and Savior Jesus Christ.

Biblically, it is helpful to understand that discipline is a key component of discipleship. Discipline is the problem-solving side of parenting that recognizes something is wrong in the heart of the child. Hebrews 12:10–11 tells us the goal of discipline is holiness that yields the fruit of peace and righteousness to those who are trained by it. God instructs parents to exercise authority over children, not for the purpose of making children do what we want, but to train children to live obediently under God's authority and learn to respect the God-ordained authority of parents, a pastor, an employer, and the governing authority (Eph. 6; Rom. 13; Heb. 13).

The early years, 1–5 years old:

◆ Read *Shepherding a Child's Heart* by Tedd Tripp and *Teach Them Diligently* by Louie Priolo to learn how to apply the biblical methods of discipline. God commands parents to discipline children (Prov. 19:18; Heb. 12:9-10; Eph. 6:4), and He didn't call parents to the task of discipline without telling us how to accomplish it.

◆ Practice obedience training in simple, enthusiastic ways. Tell your child gently that you are going to be practicing obedience. This could be done with any household activity such as picking up toys. Place a small pile of blocks on the floor. Sit with your child and explain that we are going to practice obeying mom or dad together with the blocks. When you ask your child to pick up and put away the blocks, the correct response is "Yes!" and then the child should pick up the blocks joyfully. At the moment of the child's obedience, give cheers, praise, hugs, and celebrate! Repeat this simple exercise in varying situations such as coming to you when called, sitting patiently in the cart at the grocery store, or turning off the television.

◆ Memorize Ephesians 6:1, "Children, obey your parents in the Lord for this is right." Sing along with Steve Green and the kids on Hide 'Em in Your Heart. Gently remind children of this verse when correction is needed.

◆ Establish simple household rules for expected behavior. Help your child to learn these expectations. Enforce consistent consequences for willful disobedience. Refrain from raising your voice or shouting as a consequence for disobedience.

◆ Read *Right Choices* by Kenneth Taylor together. Ask your child to identify which behaviors are right vs. wrong in the stories.

The elementary years, grades K–5:

◆ Sing and memorize the chorus of the hymn "Trust and Obey" by John H. Sammis: "Trust and obey, for there's no other way to be happy in Jesus, but to trust and obey."

◆ Memorize 1 Peter 1:14–16. Discuss why followers of Christ should desire to obey God.

◆ Identify people of authority in your child's life such as teachers, coaches, pastors, or family friends. Encourage your child to treat those people with the same respect they would give to a parent or grandparent.

◆ Read and discuss Romans 13:1–7 to understand the biblical role of government.

◆ Introduce children to your local mayor, city council, sheriff, and fire chief. Explain their roles in the city and what obeying their authority looks like.

Junior high and high school years, grades 6–12:

◆ Journey through Scripture together and learn about people who struggled with obedience. Utilize the *Obey* Bible study for teens by Kim Sorgins found at not-consumed.com.

◆ Read with your child *Ruling Over the Earth: A Biblical View of Civil Government* by Stephen McDowell.

◆ Allow independent opportunities for your child to choose obedience when you are not with them. Remind your child to obey rules and fulfill expectations even when you are not present. Follow up with your child regularly to discuss what they have been doing well and what they can improve upon in the future.

◆ When preparing for a driver's license, discuss the importance of obeying laws regarding safety and traffic signs. Look up the consequences of receiving a speeding ticket. Tell personal stories of your own experiences with not obeying roadway rules.

Make a list of your house rules. Be as detailed as you can.

_____

_____

_____

_____

_____

_____

_____

_____

_____

_____

_____

_____

_____

_____

Describe your unique ideas for teaching obedience to our child and include the date you taught them.

_____

_____

_____

_____

_____

_____

Share a memory of a time your child obeyed well.

_____
_____
_____
_____
_____

Share a memory of a time your child did not obey and the resulting consequences.

_____
_____
_____
_____
_____

Tell a story from your own childhood about a time you disobeyed and the consequences.

_____
_____
_____
_____
_____

Additional thoughts, observations, prayers or memories:

_____
_____
_____
_____
_____

KNOWS AND UNDERSTANDS
THE GOSPEL

There is nothing more important than your child knowing and understanding the Gospel, placing their faith in Jesus Christ, and then being able to share their personal testimony. Don't shy away from sharing the Gospel message early and often with your child. Charles Spurgeon exhorted parents, "Begin early to teach, for children begin early to sin." Even long after they have placed their faith in Jesus Christ, continue to remind them of His great love for them, and His sacrifice as payment for sin. Once a child has responded to the Gospel, the child can learn to share his or her testimony with others.

Tips for sharing the Gospel:

◆ Share early and often. Children need to hear the good news of Christ's life, death, and resurrection at every age and stage. There is no such thing as hearing the Gospel too often as children are prone to forget the Good News and be captivated by a gospel-replacement. Look for opportunities and confidently share. If your child has not yet placed their faith in Jesus Christ for salvation, continue to share the beauty of the Gospel and invite them to respond in faith.

◈ Give your testimony. Tell your children your conversion story. Talk about how God has changed your life and the joy of knowing Christ. There is nothing more beautiful and wonderful than the Gospel; let your children know this.

◈ Keep it simple. We've used biblical words with our children since they were little, but we always explain what they mean. Consider using concrete examples, illustrations, or tools to teach biblical truths.

◈ Don't avoid talking about sin. The Good News doesn't make sense without the bad news. We often don't give children enough credit; they can handle the truth, even at young ages.

◈ Always invite a response. When the Gospel is communicated, always invite a response, but don't manipulate a child.

◈ Be prepared to share the Gospel concisely and clearly. Become comfortable discussing key verses.

◈ Celebrate, and we mean celebrate, when a child places faith in Christ. Make it a big deal, because, what is more important in life? Plan a party to celebrate. Record the date and details so your child has a record.

◈ Pray. Pray that God will transform your child's heart. Invite others to pray with you. If your child has not come to faith, don't lose heart; continue to bring them before the Lord.

Seven resources to understand and communicate the Gospel:

◈ Purchase a children's Bible that is visually pleasing and explains the Gospel message in simple language, such as *The Big Picture Story Bible* by David R. Helm and Gail Schoonmaker, *The Jesus Storybook Bible* by Sally Lloyd-Jones and Jago, or *The Bible in Pictures for Little Eyes* by Kenneth N. Taylor. Read the Gospel story from these books. Emphasize that these stories are true.

Read the book *If Jesus Came to My House* by Joan G. Thomas, which tells the Gospel story simply and in rhyme form.

Explain the Gospel using verses from the book of Romans, sometimes referred to as Romans Road to Salvation. The problem: All have sinned (Romans 3:23). The consequence: The wages of sin is death (Romans 6:23). The solution: Christ died for us (Romans 5:8). The response: believe and repent (Romans 10:9). Sing the "Romans Road" song by Roots Kids Worship to aid in understanding and memorizing, found at GospelShapedFamily.com.

Utilize an EvangeCube to share the truth of the Gospel.

If your child is struggling with unbelief, in addition to reading the Bible with them, provide your child with books about people who have struggled in similar ways, such as *The Case for Christ* by Lee Strobel or *More Than a Carpenter* by Josh McDowell.

Place resources around the house, such as on an end table or coffee table, so that a child will see it, pick it up and read it. For younger children consider *Don't Blame the Mud: Only Jesus Makes Us Clean* by Marty Machowski and for older children utilize *What Is the Gospel?* by Greg Gilbert.

Your favorite resources used to share the Gospel with your child:

_____

_____

_____

_____

Record the date when your child responded to the Gospel. Describe the setting, who was there, and how you celebrated.

_____

_____

_____

_____

_____

_____

Write your testimony and the details of when you accepted Christ.

_____

_____

_____

_____

_____

_____

Additional thoughts, observations, prayers, or memories:

_____

_____

_____

_____

_____

_____

_____

_____

_____

OWNS A BIBLE
AND IS FAMILIAR WITH IT

A key priority for parents is to give children a Bible that fits their age and stage of development. The Bible tells us why it is important for a child to have the Word of God. The Bible is the grand instrument by which souls are converted to Jesus Christ. The mighty change is often begun by a text or doctrine of Scripture as it sinks into the heart of a child. "From childhood you have been acquainted with the sacred writings, which are able to make you wise for salvation through faith in Jesus Christ" (2 Tim. 3:15, emphasis added). God gave us the Bible to make us wise for salvation.

God caused the Bible to be "written for our instruction" (Rom. 15:4). In Psalms we find, "Since my youth, O God, you have taught me, and to this day I declare your marvelous deeds" (Ps. 71:17 NIV, emphasis added). God has declared that the Bible is "profitable" for us; 2 Timothy 3:16 also tells us that the Bible is to be used for teaching, conviction, correction, and training in righteousness. It is a sword with which all soldiers of Christ should be armed, and it is a light to our feet. It is the primary way young people are built up and established in their faith. It is the Word of God that causes growth, teaches a person how to walk in this world, and how to live to please God in all matters of life. Make it your goal to ensure that your child knows the main storyline of the Bible centered on Christ, important passages, and key people.

Give your child a Bible. There are many great options, and here are a few we recommend by age:

- **0–5**: *The Gospel Story Bible* by Marty Machowski, *The Big Picture Story Bible* by David R. Helm and Gail Schoonmaker, and *The Jesus Storybook Bible* by Sally Lloyd-Jones and Jago.

- **6–10**: *The Seek and Find Bible.* We like a full-text Bible with colorful pictures, study notes, and short articles that will interest a child.

- **11–18**: A leather-bound Bible. If you want to make it extra special, engrave your child's name on the cover.

- Consider giving your child accessories for their Bible, such as a Bible cover, tabs to quickly reference books, pigment ink pens, and a notebook to capture sermon or Bible study notes.

Make a list of Bibles your child owns and has read. Be sure to include children's Bibles, heirloom family Bibles, and their own Bible.

_____

_____

_____

_____

Record the date when your child received their own full-text Bible. What was the occasion? Who was there? What did the Bible look like? What did you write on the inside?

_____

_____

_____

_____

Share some memories of reading the Bible together. Where did you read? What time of day? How did your Bible reading times change as your child grew older?

_____

_____

_____

_____

_____

_____

_____

_____

_____

_____

Additional thoughts, observations, prayers, or memories:

_____

_____

_____

_____

_____

_____

_____

_____

_____

_____

_____

TRAINED TO WORSHIP GOD THROUGH FAMILY WORSHIP

Worship is the term we use to describe how we intentionally express the worth of God. God is worthy of our praise and worship in all times and in all places. Although it is natural to have a consciousness of God, children do not innately know God without the assistance of parents. A love for God must be awakened and explained because the mind of every child is capable of a dispassionate belief in God, and the heart is capable of focusing its affection on the wrong source.

Misdirected worship is that which fails to recognize the greatness of God. We worship God because He is a great God. Humans refrain from worshipping that which is ordinary and mundane. The not-so-great-and-impressive doesn't compel a person to worship. Even though we may have a deep affection for a loved one or a possession, we do not bow down and worship the person or thing. Why is that? The person or item lacks greatness, the one vital element inspiring worship. Therefore, one of the goals of worship in the home is to help children see and feel the greatness of God. Every child worships something—it's just a matter of what, or whom, they will serve.

Throughout church history the primary method of teaching and discipling young people has been family worship. It is the means of introducing children to the truths of Scripture and preparing children for the Christian life. The practice consists of reading the Bible as a family, praying, and praising God through music. If you have not developed the habit of regularly reading and discussing the Bible with your children, then this is a high-impact priority for you to implement.

Tips for family worship:

◈ It doesn't have to be formal or perfect. Don't strive for perfection, just start somewhere. G.K. Chesterton was known for saying, "If something is worth doing, it's worth doing badly."

◈ Read the Bible, not someone's thoughts about the Bible. The best devotionals make the Bible the primary source and keep the Gospel central to each section of Scripture. Resources include *My First Book of Questions and Answers* by Carine MacKenzie and both *Long Story Short* and *Old Story New* by Marty Machowski.

◈ Read the entire Bible to your family. The pattern of Scripture is to teach children the deep truths of Scripture. For example, children were not excused when theologically weighty topics were covered in the Colossian or Ephesian churches. Read the whole counsel of God's Word.

◈ Read briefly. Remember, they are children. Try to keep your family reading concise and to the point, but meaningful. Ten minutes is a good amount of time to begin. As children become comfortable with the habit, you can increase the length of time. The consistent habit of reading the Bible, talking about it, and making connections between what you read and everyday life makes a difference over time.

◈ If you aren't musical, use resources. Roots Kids Worship, Seeds Family Worship, and hymns are a great help. Turn on music while children play in the living room or ride in the car.

Describe what family worship looks like in your home over years. Include as many details as possible. What study books have you used? What songs did you learn tougher? How did your child's attention span and interest grow?

_____

_____

_____

What are some family worship memories, successes, or struggles?

_____

_____

_____

Additional thoughts, observations, prayers, or memories:

_____

_____

Humanity is made to worship God. Paul noted this when he visited Athens and found the citizens worshipping an unknown God. He said to these people, "I see that in every way you are very religious. As I walked around and looked carefully at your objects of worship, I even found an altar with this inscription: TO AN UNKNOWN GOD" (Acts 17:22–23 NIV). Take a moment and observe as Paul did. Walk around your child's room and observe the objects before you. What do you see? What objects of worship are displayed? What is on the wall? Is a Bible in view? What is your child filling his or her mind with? Based on what you see, what would be your child's greatest loves in life?

_____

_____

_____

_____

BAPTIZED AS A
PUBLIC EXPRESSION OF FAITH

As a pastor, there were few things that brought me greater joy than seeing a young person follow Jesus into the waters of baptism. It is a joyous occasion because the individual being baptized is publicly professing faith in Jesus Christ and wants everyone to know it! The desire to be baptized is noble and recognizes the biblical teaching that baptism is an important step of faith in a believer's life. It should not be entered into lightly or without proper preparation. Both parent and child must understand what baptism is, why a person is to be baptized, and when it is appropriate to be baptized. Baptism is often downplayed as an optional choice for the Christian. It is frequently misunderstood or minimized. Some believers view baptism as a minor addition to faith, yet the New Testament speaks of baptism as a major milestone that each and every believer in Jesus Christ is to obediently pursue. Your goal is to help your child prepare for baptism and encourage obedience in this area of life. Consider these three steps:

The first step is to determine if your child is a Christian and can articulate the Gospel message. Your job as a parent is to gauge whether or not your child is ready to be baptized.

The second step is to understand the details of baptism—the why, the what, the how, the who, and the when. Read and discuss key Bible passages together.

Your goal as a parent is to help your child understand the meaning of these passages while also providing the opportunity to let your child share his or her thoughts and feelings about baptism.

◆ **The third step** is to meet with your pastor and begin the process with your church, which may include a baptism interview, a Bible study, and the invitation for your child to write his or her testimony.

The book, *Preparing Your Child for Believer's Baptism*, available at GospelShapedFamily.com is an excellent tool to guide you through the process described above.

Tell the story of your own baptism. How old were you? Where did it take place? Who baptized you? Who was there? What were your emotions?

_____

_____

_____

_____

_____

_____

_____

Describe your child's baptism with the same detail as above.

_____

_____

_____

_____

_____

_____

_____

Ask your child to write their personal testimony to share at the time of their baptism. Keep a copy here.

How did your family celebrate the major milestone of baptism?

_____

_____

_____

_____

_____

_____

_____

Take a photo of your child being baptized. Keep a copy here.

Additional thoughts, observations, prayers, or memories:

CHAPTER 8

CHRISTLIKE
CHARACTER
DEVELOPMENT

TAUGHT THE FRUIT
OF THE SPIRIT

By nature children are patient, peaceful, unselfish, gentle, and loving. Or is that just the children raised by the family down the road or in some fantasy world from a C.S. Lewis novel? In the real world, my children throw temper tantrums in stores, walk around the house whining and crying because they couldn't wear shorts outside in the winter or were given the blue cup to drink out of instead of the green one, and can snap at others with great skill. When I'm honest, I think it's because they learned these things from me (Josh). The Bible tells us that these behaviors are the natural state of the human heart, and outward behavior change is only possible through an inward transformation of the heart. If we want to raise children who are kind, unselfish, gentle, patient, and loving, we must focus on heart transformation, which will lead to character transformation.

The fruit of the Spirit is a helpful summary of character traits that we are aiming to develop in our children, "But the fruit of the Spirit is love, joy, peace, patience, kindness, goodness, faithfulness, gentleness, self control" (Gal. 5:22–23). When our children (or we ourselves) inevitably fall short, we can gently help them understand that sin is disordered love of self rather than love for God or others. The fruit of the Spirit is not attainable through clever methods to manage behavior but is a picture of the work of the Holy Spirit in our lives, the outward manifestation of our love of Jesus Christ, and the transformation that comes with salvation. When teaching the fruit of the Spirit, be clear in communicating that these traits are not merely a checklist of skills to attain based upon good works. We cannot attain them on our own merit, but only with the help of the Holy Spirit will we imitate Christ in our actions. Our example and instruction as parents will be a faithful guide to encourage a child to pursue these Christlike characteristics.

Activities used to teach the fruit of the Spirit:

- Read Galatians 5:22–23 to your child. Pray together that the Lord would cultivate the fruit of the Spirit in their lives.

- Memorize the nine fruits by saying them together or singing "The Fruit of the Spirit" song by Go Fish.

- Artfully display the fruits of the Spirit in your home. Websites such as Etsy have many options to suit your style and budget.

- Plant a fruit-bearing tree in your yard with your child. Water and fertilize it together. As fruit grows and is ready for harvest, explain that good fruit comes from a healthy plant. Similarly, we show the fruit of the Spirit in our own lives when the source is our relationship with Jesus Christ.

- Pack *Fruit of the Spirit Conversation Cards* from the Tiny Theologians website in your purse or car's glove compartment. Pull them out to spark conversation during drives to and from school, church, or activities.

- Set aside a week to emphasize each of the nine fruits of the Spirit as a family. During that time, be intentional to notice the emphasized weekly trait in your child and in others. As a family, be creative in keeping track of what you observe!

Use a jar with a lid and slips of paper. Encourage family members to write down examples they see of each other displaying that particular fruit. At the end of the week, read the contents of the jar out loud.

A time I observed in you

Christlike love:

_____

_____

_____

_____

Vibrant joy:

_____

_____

_____

_____

Peace in the midst of trials:

_____

_____

_____

_____

_____

Patience:

_____

_____

_____

_____

_____

Kindness to others:

_____
_____
_____
_____

Goodness (doing what is right and good in the eyes of God):

_____
_____
_____
_____

Faithfulness:

_____
_____
_____
_____

Gentleness:

_____
_____
_____
_____

Self-control:

_____
_____
_____
_____

TRAINED TO SERVE OTHERS

Serving others is critical because it puts an end to selfishness that reigns in all of our hearts. Our children must learn to control their passions through disciplined living and an others-centered mindset. Serving is the antidote to the poison of self-centeredness common in our culture, which teaches that satisfying our desires is the key to the good life. The Christian learns that true happiness is living in harmony with God's commands and serving others.

Jesus told us that He came to serve others, and we see this best displayed with a towel and wash basin and ultimately on the cross. To be great in God's kingdom is to be a servant to others. While serving can be fun and feel good, it should be motivated by love and seen as an outward expression of faith in Christ. Children are able to serve the people around them in meaningful, impactful ways, even from the youngest age. "Each one should use whatever gift he has received to serve others, faithfully administering God's grace in its various forms" (I Pet. 4:10 NIV). Training your child to serve develops the lifelong skill of working hard, but also shapes tender hearts to use their talents for the glory of God and the aid of others.

The early years:

- As soon as children are able to follow simple instructions they are able to serve. Get creative with ways little hands can serve God and their community.

◆ Pick up! Organize a group of friends or your child's Sunday school class to pick up stray landscape rocks from church landscaping, pull weeds from gardens, or clean up under pews or seats after church gatherings.

◆ Create artwork to share with pastors, grandparents, teachers, and community leaders.

◆ Serve together as a family. Greet guests at church, take meals to families in need, or do yard work for elderly neighbors. Involve your little ones as much as possible.

The elementary years:

◆ Serving begins at home. We have a saying in our family, "See a need, meet a need." We aim to cultivate a willing spirit, a helpful attitude, and faith that is manifested in action through genuine service to one another.

◆ Serve together at your church. Whether you are ushering or taking care of babies in the nursery, model joyful service to your child.

◆ Memorize I Peter 4:10 together. Encourage your child with this verse when you see them serving.

◆ Give ample opportunities for your child to serve others throughout the year. Each season will present unique opportunities. Make serving together the culture of your family and be willing to say yes when opportunities arise.

The older years:

◆ Take a mission trip together. Serving God and others on a missions trip will demand service at a deeper level, make the Gospel come alive, and may even be the means God uses to call your child into vocational ministry.

◆ Older siblings can serve younger one by helping meet needs, make meals, and by babysitting.

◆ We've made it a priority to attend church for two hours on Sunday morning so that our children can worship corporately one hour and serve the second hour, which has resulted in our children loving their church and owning their faith.

◆ Invite older children to join you in your area of serving and make them your "ministry associate" with meaningful tasks. I (Josh) invite children to accompany me when I travel and speak. They welcome guests, set up our booth, distribute materials, and run the table.

Does your child serve at church or in the community? If so, describe what they do. If not, brainstorm with your child ways to serve together.

_____

_____

_____

_____

_____

_____

In what ways have you modeled a life of service to your child?

_____

_____

_____

_____

_____

_____

Tell about a special memory of your child's service, or of serving together.

_____
_____
_____
_____
_____
_____
_____

Additional thoughts, observations, prayers, or memories:

_____
_____
_____
_____
_____
_____
_____
_____
_____
_____
_____

TAUGHT TO
UNDERSTAND SUFFERING

My dad and I carried my mother into my home because she couldn't walk up the stairs. She had just finished meeting with the neurologist at the Mayo Clinic, a few blocks from our house, and had stopped by to tell us the results. I sat there stunned when she said, "I have ALS and the doctors give me two to three years to live." Turns out, she died six months later. ALS, or amyotrophic lateral sclerosis, causes neurons in the brain to deteriorate so that messages don't get sent to the muscles, which causes paralysis. It's a painful, horrible way to die.

After receiving the news I wrote a message to the congregation I pastored:

I often remind you that God is sovereign and in control, faithful, and our Rock. I continually say that storms in life will come, along with suffering and hard times; if you have not experienced them yet, you will at some time. I also talk about how it would be a foolish act to turn our back on God in the hard times in life because that is when we need Him most and will come to know Him better. Recently, God has given me the opportunity to grow in faith and live what I preach.

I could say these words because my parents prepared me to suffer. When suffering came, as it will for your child, it didn't destroy my faith but became an opportunity to grow in holiness and glorify God. What your child believes before suffering is critical to help them when suffering comes. Here are six principles they need to learn to suffer well:

1. God created the world good, but it was broken due to sin. The world is not as it should be. Death, disease, natural disasters, broken homes, and injustice are a result of the fall. Suffering and pain came into the world through sin (Rom. 8:20). All creation groans (Rom. 8:22–23).

2. Everyone suffers because we live in a broken world, so don't be surprised when suffering comes. John 16:33 reminds us, "In the world you will have tribulation." Those who trust Jesus should expect to suffer even more. Jesus told his followers, "If they persecuted me, they will also persecute you" (John 15:20). In a post-Christian world, children need to be prepared to be mistreated for their faith in Christ. God does not promise us prosperity, but he does tell us to expect suffering and persecution.

3. God is good and sovereign. Children need to be saturated with the nature and character of God. What they believe about who God is will fortify their faith against the corrosive power of suffering. Children need to believe that suffering does not exist because God is helpless or unloving. God is good and in control. This is true in good times and in difficult times. Most of the time we will not understand why we suffer, so asking why is often a fruitless exercise.

4. Proclaim the Gospel. God sent His Son into the world to suffer with us and to suffer for us. For those who trust in Christ, suffering refines us and helps us grow in Christlikeness. Suffering can lead to some of the most intimate times with God and growth in holiness.

5. A day is coming when there will be no more suffering. God will make all things new and it is a day we can look forward to with great hope! There will be no more pain, no more tears, no more sorrow, no more injustice, and no more death (Rev. 21:4–5). If it looks like evil is triumphing or that someone is getting away with something unjust, we can have confidence that God will bring that person to justice in judgment. "Vengeance is mine, I will repay, says the Lord" (Rom. 12:19). Because we know a better day is coming and that suffering is only temporary, we can have serenity in our heart in the midst of the storm.

6. We should model trust and hope in the midst of our own suffering. My mother taught me as much in her suffering and death as she did in her living. The apostle Paul instructed Timothy to follow his example of faith and steadfastness in suffering and stated, "All who desire to live a godly life in Christ Jesus will be persecuted . . . continue in what you have learned and firmly believe" (2 Tim. 3:10–14). Our children are watching how we suffer. The Bible tells us how to respond: "We rejoice in our sufferings" (Rom. 5:3) and "Count it joy, my brothers, when you meet trials of various kinds" (Jas. 1:2). Nothing will be more powerful than your example in suffering.

Describe a time in your own life when you experienced suffering. How did the Lord comfort and sustain you through that difficult time?

_____

_____

_____

_____

_____

_____

_____

_____

Has your child experienced suffering or loss? If so, how have you equipped them to suffer well? How will you intentionally model trust and hope to your child?

_____

_____

_____

_____

_____

_____

Additional thoughts, observations, prayers, or memories:

_____

_____

_____

_____

_____

_____

_____

_____

_____

LEARNED PERSONAL
RESPONSIBILITY

Jen and I decided that our children were getting old enough to leave them home alone for short periods of time, so we thought that a fifteen-minute walk down our country gravel road would be a good place to start. We told our children, "You have one job—safety! Make sure everyone is safe." It seemed simple enough, and we thought, "What can go wrong in fifteen minutes when we are only a couple blocks away?" Turns out, a lot can go wrong. When we turned into the driveway at the conclusion of the walk, Asher came bursting out the back door, screaming at the top of his lungs, holding a rag over his mouth. When he removed the rag, tooth chunks fell to the ground. After we left, the children decided to play baseball. In the house. With a full-sized bat and ball. Asher was hit in the mouth with the bat when he was rounding third, headed for home, and his sister had a major league-worthy bat flip after a solid single. Our children didn't do so well with the small responsibility they were given. It was a teachable moment for our children. We talked about how freedom comes with responsibility and those who are responsible with little are often entrusted with more responsibility. We spent thousands of dollars to repair Asher's tooth, but the repair always breaks off, leaving Asher with half of a front tooth. It is a visual reminder to our children that irresponsible decisions are costly and can be lifelong. God has used that experience, and our children have grown in personal responsibility.

Responsibility is learned through the combination of age-appropriate opportunity plus accountability. It is an art for parents to determine how much responsibility a child is ready to handle. We've tried to avoid two opposite ends of the spectrum, giving a child too much responsibility too early or not enough responsibility for their age or maturity level. Responsibility is the fruit of accepting ownership for something and is displayed through initiative, dependability, and quality effort. Children are by nature irresponsible, so parents need to be prepared to provide unconditional love and see failure as an opportunity for growth. We've also learned to celebrate small successes when a child is responsible, as this builds confidence, encourages the child to take good risks and believe they are capable of accomplishing difficult tasks. When a child is young, the parent does everything for the child. Over time, responsibility needs to be transferred to the child so that by the time the child leaves home, he or she is responsible with time, tasks, money, and the demands of an adult life. The ultimate goal is self-government, the ability to exercise all functions without the intervention from an external authority. The opportunities to teach children responsibility are endless—every task, whether small or large, is a building block to teach a child responsibility.

Make a list of specific freedoms you gave your child with the intention of teaching personal responsibility.

_____

_____

_____

_____

What successes and/or failures did your child experience while learning personal responsibility?

_____

_____

_____

_____

Additional thoughts, observations, prayers, or memories:

_____
_____
_____
_____
_____
_____
_____
_____
_____
_____
_____
_____

GIVES AND RECEIVES FORGIVENESS FREELY

ndrew and Amy's marriage was hanging on by a thread, and they contacted me as a last resort. The first meeting in my office was equivalent to an hour-long boxing match during which each of them brought up years of marital hurt, resentment, and pain. Things had gotten so bad that they slept in different rooms, could barely communicate without shouting, and were ready to sign divorce papers. Andrew and Amy had never learned to forgive others, and that had slowly corroded their marriage. They experienced a simple truth: Unforgiveness always leads to bitterness, and bitterness leads to anger. Once Andrew and Amy learned to apply the biblical principles of forgiveness to their marriage, it steadily improved, and today they are still married and growing in intimacy. Broken or damaged relationships are greatly affected by ungodly responses to offenses, hurts, and accumulated grudges.

Do you want your child to have healthy and godly relationships as an adult? A willingness to forgive is essential to maintaining healthy relationships. No parent expects to have an estranged relationship with an adult child or to raise a child whose marriage ends in divorce, yet these experiences are common. What we do as parents today to train our children to navigate conflict and forgive family and friends will impact their most important relationships in the future.

Forgiveness is at the very heart of the Gospel and it is central in all relationships. The biblical antidote for conflict is the healing power of forgiveness. To understand forgiveness we must appreciate the depth to which we have been forgiven by Jesus. Someone who understands how much they have been forgiven by God will forgive others with the same measure of grace. Take a moment and praise God for cancelling your sin debt and for forgiveness through Christ! "Blessed are those whose lawless deeds are forgiven, and whose sins are covered" (Rom. 4:7). We must teach our children to forgive others as they have been forgiven by God. A recognition of our need for forgiveness from God will produce a humility and tenderness of heart to forgive others and confess our own sin. The Bible has a lot to say about forgiveness and this would be a valuable study between parent and child. Here are some key principles to apply to your home:

Principles of forgiveness to model and teach a child:

1. *Forgiveness is to be modeled after God's forgiveness.* "Bear with each other and forgive one another if any of you has a grievance against someone. Forgive as the Lord forgave you" (Col. 3:13 NIV). God forgives unconditionally (Rom. 5:8), completely (Ps. 103:12), and with kindness and compassion (Eph. 4:32). We are to do the same.

2. *Forgiveness cancels a debt.* Forgiveness requires that someone bear the cost of what is owed. If you are having a hard time forgiving, remember that it is not our role to make someone pay for a wrong. We release this to God, who ultimately will make all things right.

3. *Forgiveness is a choice.* Forgiveness does not mean you forget. God knows our sin; He chooses not to hold it against us.

4. *Forgiveness makes a three-fold promise:* (1) I will not bring up this offense again or use it against you. (2) I will not gossip or malign you because of the offense. (3) I will not dwell on the offense.

5. *Forgiveness is both an event and process.* It takes time to heal. Forgiveness does not change feelings immediately. Every time I forgive someone it is an event: "I forgive you." Every time I remember the offense I need to continue to forgive and resist my sinful desire for revenge.

Spend some time with your child reading Bible passages that teach about forgiveness. What passages did you read? What observations did your child make?

_____

_____

_____

Describe a time when your child needed to ask forgiveness from another person. What were the circumstances? Did the other person freely offer forgiveness? How did your child feel before and after resolution?

_____

_____

Share a memory of time you asked for forgiveness from your child. How did your relationship deepen as a result?

_____

_____

Additional thoughts, observations, prayers, or memories:

_____

_____

_____

_____

CHAPTER 9

BIBLICAL BELIEFS AND WORLDVIEW

TAUGHT CORE DOCTRINE OF SCRIPTURE

The pattern of Scripture is for children of all ages to be taught the core truths of the Bible so that they will be firmly rooted in Christ and established in their faith (Col. 2:7). God's instructions for parents are clear: "You shall teach them diligently to your children" (Deut. 6:7) and "bring them up in the discipline and instruction of the Lord" (Eph. 6:4). We do this anticipating that 3 John 1:4 will be true for our children, "I have no greater joy than to hear that my children are walking in the truth."

Many Christian children are biblically illiterate; they know more about athletes than the Bible. Errors arise from ignorance of the Bible. There are countless young people who know little about the Gospel, the exclusiveness of Christ, the commands of God, or the contents of the Scriptures. Many young people cannot explain its core teachings and have little idea of the meaning of faith, conversion, justification, and sanctification. As a result, false teachings are not identified and indifference to false doctrine reigns. The Bible clearly states what will happen to children when they are not well grounded in God's Word. Children are taken captive by man's ideas and deceived by human traditions (Col. 2:8). Children grow up not knowing God or His great works

(Judg. 2:10). Make it your goal to ensure that your child knows the core doctrines of the Christian faith including the Bible, the nature and character of God the Father, Jesus Christ, the Holy Spirit, humanity, salvation, the church, angels, and Satan, the last things, as well as areas of Christian living such as marriage, family, education, and government.

The primary way to accomplish this task is to read through the Bible as a family and discuss the truths in the text. The Bible is your primary curriculum as a parent. Historically, one of the common methods to teach children the core truths of the Christian faith has been a catechism. A catechism is simply systematic instruction using a question-and-answer format based on a key passage of Scripture. Here are some ideas for using a catechism with your family:

- Choose a catechism that centers on the Gospel and main storyline of Scripture. The Heidelberg Catechism (1576) and Westminster Shorter Catechism (1647) are good options and have been widely used through history. These catechisms teach the storyline of Scripture, creation, rebellion, and redemption, as well as the Apostles' Creed, the Ten Commandments, and Lord's Prayer.

- Choose a catechism that fits the age and stage of your child. *My First Book of Questions and Answers* by Carine MacKenzie is great for those in preschool and early grade school. *The New City Catechism* by Kathy Keller is great for older grade school children and teenagers.

- Recognize that a catechism is secondary, not primary. Your primary text is the Bible. A good catechism drives you to Scripture. Don't make a catechism your main tool. Use it as a supplement to your regular family Scripture reading.

- If you have older and younger children, allow your oldest to lead the catechism discussion. We often hand a catechism book to an older child and ask him or her to choose three questions and lead the conversation. Not only do they learn in the process, but they get to practice how to lead family worship, and it keeps them engaged.

♦ As children move into the teen years, purchase more meaty books on doctrine for them to read. A few examples include *Essential Truths of the Christian Faith* by R.C. Sproul, *The Whole Message of the Bible in 16 Words* by Chris Bruno, and when your child is ready to dive deep, *Systematic Theology* by Wayne Grudem.

How have you made it a priority to teach the core doctrine of Scripture to your child? What resources did you use?

_____

_____

_____

_____

_____

Use the space below to write key doctrines you would like to teach your child in the coming years:

_____

_____

_____

_____

_____

Additional thoughts, observations, prayers, or memories:

_____

_____

_____

_____

_____

_____

KNOWS THE WHY OF FAITH
AND CAN DEFEND BELIEFS

Young people are more likely to remain faithful to a faith they understand and can defend. In a post-Christian culture, it is more critical than ever for young people to know what they believe, why they believe it, and be prepared to defend themselves from attacks to their faith. Throughout church history this has been known as apologetics. Apologetics is the defense of the Christian faith. Peter states that Christians are to be prepared "to make a defense to everyone who asks you to give an account for the hope that is in you" (1 Pet. 3:15 NASB). A portion of Paul's ministry included a defense of the Gospel: "I am appointed for a defense of the gospel" (Phil. 1:16 NASB). Apologists are individuals who defend Christian beliefs and practices against attacks, provide arguments for the truthfulness of Christianity over other worldviews, and refute unbiblical ideas or theories. The goal of apologetics is to persuade belief by presenting a rational basis for Christianity, to defend the truth by answering questions or the objections of unbelief, and to reveal the foolishness of false ideas so they do not capture the heart and mind of our children. Apologetics can be divided into the following four categories:

 Prove. Develop a case for Christianity utilizing biblical, scientific, historical, archeological, and personal testimony to establish the truthfulness of the

Christian worldview. Show that Christianity is true, credible, reliable, and aligns with the real world.

Defend. In every generation there are many attacks against Christianity, and children need to be introduced to these distorted ideas, learn to test them against God's Word, and be able to identify truth from error. The two primary areas of attack: the Son of God and the Word of God.

Refute. Compare and contrast with other religions and belief systems to verify the Chrisitan faith and dismantle false and erroneous views. Refute arguments made in support of different beliefs by showing they are unreliable, irrational, unverifiable, or simply do not make sense with what we see in real life.

Persuade. Work to clarify biblical truths, answer objections, address criticisms, provide answers and eliminate any intellectual difficulties that stand in the way of coming to faith in Christ. The goal is to encourage alignment with God's Word, apply the truth of God's Word to life, and establish a lifelong commitment to the Gospel. Apologetics is a partner of evangelism where we seek to convince children to accept truth claims about Christianity and trust Christ. Give your child every reason possible to embrace the Christian faith and reject counterfeit beliefs.

Six tips to help children understand and defend their faith:

Utilize questions to grow the faith of future generations. Your goal is twofold: to become an askable parent and to become skilled at the art of asking good questions. Use questions to create serious spiritual dialogue, to encourage critical thinking, and to discover what children believe.

Take objections from children seriously. Do not mock an objection or dismiss a question. Spend as much time and energy as needed to fully explore a topic with a child.

💎 *Anticipate attacks and arguments that a child will face in the teen and adult years.* After teaching a biblical truth to a child, present the faulty argument to a child, prove why it is false, give reading materials that establish the truth, and continue to point out in conversation over the years the erroneous arguments.

💎 *Build an apologetics library for each child.* These make great gifts. Suggested books include *Cold-Case Christianity* by J. Warner Wallace, *Tactics* by Gregory Koukl, *Answers Vols. 1–4* by Answers in Genesis, *Quick Answers to Social Issues* by Bryan Osborne, *Demolishing Supposed Bible Contradictions* by Ken Ham, *Debunking Evolution* by Dr. Daniel A. Biddle, *True For You But Not for Me* by Paul Copan, and *The Case for Christ* by Lee Strobel. Research other books and tools that will help your children build and defend their faith. Use the planning tool at the end of the book to help you in this area.

💎 *Expose your children to the truth in real-life experiences.* Allow children to see a live ultrasound so they learn the horrors of abortion, visit the Creation Museum to teach the truth of creation and then visit a natural history museum to show the error of evolution, or travel to Israel together to see the accuracy, reliability, and truthfulness of the Bible.

💎 *Look for examples of false beliefs or erroneous messages in movies, music, books, and television.* Point them out, ask questions, and discuss why something is problematic. Always point back to Scripture so that it is not your opinion, but based on the authority of God's Word.

Tell about a time you were able to help your child analyze their faith in comparison to a message they received in real-life situations, such as at school or in media:

_____

_____

_____

What topics did you address through the years to help build and defend your child's faith?

Ages 0–5:

_____

_____

_____

Ages 6–10:

_____

_____

_____

Ages 11–14:

_____

_____

_____

Ages 15–18:

_____

_____

_____

Additional thoughts, observations, prayers, or memories:

_____

_____

_____

_____

DEVELOPED A
BIBLICAL WORLDVIEW

Worldviews are like belly buttons—everyone has one. Every child will develop a worldview; the question is whether it will be biblical, a different world religion, or secular. With a secular worldview, the culture dictates how a child should think, act, and live. A biblical worldview is developed when the Bible dictates what a child believes and how a child lives. A complete biblical worldview is the Gospel, based on the Bible's big story, developed by teaching young people the whole counsel of the Word of God, and living as a Christlike example worthy of imitation. The goal of worldview training is to shape beliefs with the Bible to equip a young person to apply God's truth to every area of life for the good of others and the glory of God.

What a young person believes *about* the Bible is a matter of utmost importance. A battle exists for the Bible. The world wants to destroy the authority and trustworthiness of the Bible and distort its truth in the eyes of our children, which is why we must work diligently to establish the Bible's authority, prove its reliability, show its trustworthiness, and apply its usefulness to all of life. Every young person will ask three questions about the Bible: Is it true? Does it apply? Will I follow? We must diligently work to answer these questions and persuade a child to embrace the authority and sufficiency of Scripture.

We must train young people to love God's Word, trust God's Word, and live by God's Word. A child may not know the answer to a question, but if we teach a child to study the Bible, he or she will know where to look to find the answer. A biblical worldview is developed as we train young people to ask, "What does the Bible say about _____?"

Resources to help children develop a biblical worldview:

💎 As a parent, read *Biblical Worldview: What It Is, Why It Matters and How to Shape the Worldview of the Next Generation* by Josh Mulvihill.

💎 Have an older grade school student read and fill out the workbook in *What Does the Bible Say about That?* by Kevin Swanson.

💎 Have a high school student read *How Should We Then Live?* by Francis Schaeffer and *Total Truth* by Nancy Pearcey.

💎 Have a high school student take a biblical worldview assessment called *The ViewFinder* available at Renewanation.org and utilize the accompanying e-book, *Essentials of a Biblical Worldview* to discuss thirty biblical worldview topics with your teenager.

💎 Listen to *The Christian Worldview* radio program by David Wheaton and the *Worldview Weekend* radio program by Brannon Howse to help a young person learn to think biblically about cultural events.

💎 Research other books and resources you plan to use to help train your children or teenager with a biblical worldview.

Share an example of when you discussed a biblical view of the following topics with your child. Record the date and context. What additional questions did your child have?

Truth:

_____
_____
_____
_____

Creation:

_____
_____
_____
_____

Morality:

_____
_____
_____
_____

Government:

_____
_____
_____
_____
_____

Family:

_____
_____
_____
_____

Church:

_____

_____

_____

Education:

_____

_____

_____

Economics:

_____

_____

_____

Humanity:

_____

_____

_____

Sexuality:

_____

_____

_____

Additional thoughts, observations, prayers, or memories:

_____

_____

_____

DEVELOPED A BIBLICAL VIEW
OF MANHOOD AND WOMANHOOD

Parents have the wonderful privilege of providing a godly example and a clear vision of what it means to become a godly man or woman. Biblical manhood and womanhood is about Christlike character and God-designed roles. Men and women are both created in the image of God and are equal in value and dignity, but they have distinct roles in the home and church. For men, the role involves servant leadership as well as protection and provision. For women, it's about being a willing helpmate through management, nurture, and support. Boys can be trained for manhood using the question, "How can I serve you?" and girls can be trained for womanhood using the question, "How can I help you?" The reality is that men and women are not born, boys and girls are. Becoming a godly man or woman requires instruction and example.

In the words of Paul, we want our children to "do away with the childish things" and, as the book of 1 Chronicles describes, we want our sons to grow up to become like the men of Asher who were "heads of families, choice men, brave warriors and outstanding leaders" (1 Chron. 7:40 NIV). The Bible says in Titus 2:4–5 that older women, which applies to mothers and grandmothers, are to "train the young women to love their husbands and children, to be self-controlled, pure, working at home, kind, and submissive to their own husbands." If God specifically tells moms to teach something to their daughters, then it's important! Let's provide our children with a clear, biblical, God-honoring vision of what it means to be a man or woman and provide other godly role models for our children to be around and learn from.

Manhood and womanhood are in a state of confusion and under attack. Children are being influenced by the misguided thinking of our culture, which fails to acknowledge this basic truth: Boys and girls are different. Media often depict men as either adrenaline-loving, responsibility-ignoring rebels or weak-willed, decision-avoidant effeminates. Women are depicted as strong-willed, career-minded feminists or body-flaunting aggressors. This unbiblical picture of manhood and womanhood is troubling. Some groups have declared an all-out war on boyhood and girlhood by trying to blur the lines between men and women and redefine gender identity, male and female roles, as well as masculinity and femininity. Society has rejected God's design for men and woman and has tried to create their own version of a genderless identity. The cultural messages in this area of life are strong, and without intentional training and godly examples, our sons and daughters can easily adopt unbiblical thinking and the sinful practices of our time.

Five resources to teach biblical manhood and womanhood

As a parent, it is important that you equip yourself with a healthy knowledge of biblical manhood and womanhood so you can teach this to your child. A resource that equips parents to teach both boys and girls, *Preparing Children for Marriage* by Josh Mulvihill has sections on teaching biblical manhood and womanhood to a child. Additional helpful resources include *True Woman 101* by Mary A. Kassian and Nancy Leigh DeMoss, *Love Thy Body* by Nancy R. Pearcy, *8 Great Dates for Moms and Daughters* by Dannah Gresh, *Future Men* by Douglas Wilson and *Thoughts for Young Men* by J.C. Ryle.

Ideas to teach manhood and womanhood

- Provide your child toys that affirm their biological sex. Give girls dolls, aprons, and play kitchens. Give your boys trucks, cars, tools, and nerf guns.

- Play dress up! Little children love to dress in costumes. Encourage your child to enjoy creative play that affirms their biological sex with princess dresses, tiaras, and sparkly shoes for girls, and cowboy hats, boots, and knight costumes for boys. Be creative!

Verbally encourage your child in ways that affirm gender roles. Tell your daughter she will be an excellent wife and mother. Tell your son he will be an outstanding leader, husband, and father.

In the teen years, give your child gifts they will use as future adult men and women. Examples include Bible commentaries and study volumes, a wallet, tools, a gun, or hunting and fishing gear for young men. For young women, consider Bible commentaries and books, jewelry and jewelry box, a timeless purse, cookbooks, or kitchen tools.

Celebrate your child's unique giftings. Not all boys love sports and guns. Not all girls enjoy playing with dolls and wearing tutus. Many voices in society will use a child's preferences to fuel a narrative that children who do not fit stereotypical molds are transgender or are still discovering their gender. Do not heed this advice. Instead, give your child examples of men and women who love God and have served Him well while not fitting the mold of stereotypes, such as Annie Lawson, Mildred Cable, C.S. Lewis, and Samuel Morse. Teach your child to use their distinct preferences, talents and skills to enhance the way they serve God uniquely as male and female.

After studying biblical manhood and womanhood on a deeper level, what did you learn? How did your study affirm or contrast with what you were taught about manhood and womanhood as a young person? What key truths do you want to teach your child?

Record toys, gifts, and resources you gave your child to encourage their manhood or womanhood:

Ages 0–5:

_____

_____

Ages 6–10:

_____

_____

Ages 11–14:

_____

_____

Ages 15–18:

_____

_____

Make a list of qualities you see in our child that affirm their God-given qualities as male and female:

_____

_____

_____

Additional thoughts, observations, prayers, or memories:

_____

_____

_____

DEVELOPED A BASIC UNDERSTANDING OF CHURCH HISTORY

Studying church history is learning the stories, trials, sacrifices, and joys of those who have come before us in our Christan walk. The heroes of the Christian faith led daring, bold lives that were anything but dull or boring. They teach us how to live faithful, obedient, and courageous lives for the glory of God. Learning church history should not be an exercise in memorizing timelines and charts, but instead the experience of becoming immersed in an engaging, exciting true adventure. In teaching church history to our own children, we have found that reading excellent biographies has been the best way to make church history come alive. Utilize biographies by either reading them aloud to your children or giving them to your child as a gift. Once your child reads one, they will want to read more! If you desire, pair biographes with a beautifully illustrated timeline. A printed timeline gives context to see when events took place without the pressure to memorize details. If you are not familiar with church history, do not shy away from learning it alongside your child.

Excellent biographies for experiencing church history with your child:

◆ Church history board books by Rebecca VanDoodewaard. Ages 1–3

◆ Little Lights series by Catherine MacKenzie. Ages 3–7

◈ *She Believed* and *She Prayed* by Jean Fischer. Ages 5+

◈ Christian Biographies for Young Readers series by Simonetta Carr. Ages 5+

◈ The Torchbearers series by Catherine Mackenzie. Ages 7+

◈ Ten Boys and Ten Girls series by Irene Howat. Ages 8+

◈ The Torchlighters series. Ages 8+

◈ Trail Blazers series by Christian Focus Publishers. Ages 10+

◈ Hidden Heroes series by Rebecca Davis, Ages 10+

◈ History Lives series by Brandon Withrow and Mindy Withrow. Ages 10+

◈ *Christian History Made Easy* by Timothy Paul Jones. Ages 12+

Additional resources to bring church history alive:

◈ Take a vacation to important places in church history either in the United States or abroad. When I (Josh) was a young adult, I took a church history trip to England and visited Spurgeon's church, Wesley's home, C.S. Lewis's home, the birthplace of Sunday School, and many more sites that made church history come alive.

◈ Purchase a timeline such as *The Rose Book of Bible & Christian History Time Lines* by Rose Publishing to make the connection between what events happened and when.

◈ Many of the greatest stories in church history have been adapted into movies or television shows. The Torchlighters animated series is excellent for children.

Older teens would benefit from full motion pictures such as *The Hiding Place* or *Joni*, the Joni Eareckson Tada story. Preview any media before allowing your children to watch it and watch a movie together as a family to aid with discussion and shared connection.

◆ Discuss church history events throughout the year. Recognize important dates when they occur, such as Reformation Day, Pentecost Sunday, Ash Wednesday, Maundy Thursday, and others.

Still don't know where to begin? Make your own top-ten list of influential people in church history. Find a book or movie about that person and go! The following is a sample list for you:

1. Augustine
2. John Wesley
3. John Bunyan
4. William Tyndale
5. George Mueller
6. Amy Carmichael
7. Corrie ten Boom
8. Jim Elliott
9. Francis and Edith Schaeffer
10. Martin Luther

Make a list of people in church history you would like to learn about with your child.

_____

_____

_____

_____

List the books you read and movies you watched together to learn about church history. Record the date and what you learned:

_____

_____

_____

_____

Activities we did to make church history come alive:

_____
_____
_____
_____
_____

Who are your child's favorite people in church history and why?

_____
_____
_____
_____
_____

Additional thoughts, observations, prayers, or memories:

_____
_____
_____
_____
_____
_____
_____
_____
_____

All these were descendants of Asher—
heads of families, choice men, brave
warriors and outstanding leaders.
The number of men ready for battle,
as listed in their genealogy, was 26,000.

1 Chronicles 7:40

CHAPTER 10

SPIRITUAL GROWTH

KNOWS HOW TO STUDY THE
BIBLE AND HAVE DAILY DEVOTIONS

During the early years of a child's life, the parent is the one to feed the child spiritually. But gradually this responsibility should be shifted to the child. For this to happen, parents must teach their child how to read the Bible and develop a pattern of daily devotions. Children learn about the value of daily Bible reading and study by seeing parents model reading God's Word. Children should be taught basic Bible study methods, which include observation, interpretation, and application. This is known as inductive Bible study.

- *Observation:* We ask, "What does this passage say?" Observation is taking a close look at what is going on in the passage of Scripture. Correct observations are key to understanding the meaning of the text. We need to read the Bible thoroughly, slowly, and prayerfully to understand what God is saying.

- *Interpretation:* We ask, "What does this mean?" Interpretation is trying to understand the intent of the author. Interpretation is affected by the culture in which the author wrote, the biases we bring to the text, and the context in which the passage is found. We cannot understand a verse without understanding a chapter. We cannot understand a chapter without understanding the entire book. We should teach children to interpret Scripture with Scripture and to consult resources such as commentaries to best understand a passage. Questions that help us understand a passage include: What is good about God in this passage? What is rotten about humanity or needs to be repaired in the world? What is taught about Jesus?

Application: We ask, "What does this passage require of me?" and "What wisdom is taught that can be applied to life?" We come to the Bible for transformation, not simply information. God's Word has the authority to tell us how to live. We train children to obey all God's commands, not just the ones they like. Teach children that obedience is essential, not optional.

Resources to help children learn how to study the Bible. For younger children, we've utilized *How to Study Your Bible for Kids* by Kay Arthur and Janna Arndt and *Exploring the Bible* by David Murray. For older children we have used *How to Study the Bible* by John MacArthur. Groups such as Bible Study Fellowship also offer excellent resources for learning to study the Bible for both young people and adults.

Provide Bible study tools for older children. Every child should know how to use tools to help them understand the Bible. These reference books make great gifts for teenage children. Consider building a reference library for each child utilizing the following items:

Commentaries: A commentary simply explains the meaning and application of Scripture. Scholars spend great amounts of time studying the Bible. They write about their discoveries in commentaries. Scripture can be difficult to understand, so good commentaries are helpful for a young person.

Bible dictionary: A Bible dictionary lists items by theme. Using this tool, young people will be taught to look up people, places, and themes of Scripture.

Bible dictionaries help a person quickly learn about important and obscure people of the Bible or the meaning of a word. Children can also look up themes such as faith and learn more about the topic.

◆ *Concordance:* A concordance is a catalog of the Bible. It lists every word in alphabetical order and tells where to find each word by listing references. It is extremely helpful if a young person wants to study a specific word or remembers a word in a passage but cannot remember the reference.

◆ *Bible atlas:* A Bible atlas will teach about the geography of the Bible, the location of cities, and the whereabouts of important happenings. For example, there is an Old Testament Jericho and a New Testament Jericho. This is helpful to understand.

Let us remember that it is one thing to *have* a Bible, another thing to *read* it, yet most important to *live* it. We are persuaded that many young people have a Bible, but never read it. It sits on a shelf, a stand, or in a book bag. It collects dust and is in pristine condition. Neglect of the Bible is like disease to the body. Every living thing requires food. Our body needs food to sustain and nourish it. It is equally so with our spiritual life. The only food that will sustain and nourish our child's soul is the Word of God.

Our aim should be to raise children who are mighty in the Scriptures just like the Bereans: "Now these Jews were more noble than those in Thessalonica; they received the word with all eagerness, examining the Scriptures daily to see if these things were so" (Acts 17:11).

Describe your own daily devotions and Bible reading. Use as much detail as you can. What do you read? What time of day do you read? Where do you sit? How has your routine changed over time and in different seasons of life?

_____

_____

_____

What are some of the most meaningful passages of Scripture to you?
Record those here for your child:

_____

_____

_____

Set aside a time to show your child how to use a concordance, Bible dictionary,
commentary, and atlas. Describe how these tools helped the Bible come alive
for you and your child:

_____

_____

_____

In what ways did you facilitate your child's daily Bible reading?
What resources did you provide them with to aid their study?

_____

_____

_____

Additional thoughts, observations, prayers, or memories:

_____

_____

_____

_____

_____

_____

_____

_____

KNOWS HOW TO PRAY

Natalie and her mom had just finished their counseling appointment with me. I asked Natalie to close our time in prayer, which I thought was a small request. Turns out I was wrong. I bowed my head and waited for the eighth-grader to speak. Instead of a prayer, I sat there for a long awkward silence. After what felt like an eternity, I tilted my head up and peaked to see what Natalie was doing. She was staring at me with wide open eyes and exclaimed, "I've never prayed out loud before. I don't know how to do it." Upon further discussion, I learned that her parents had never taught her to pray.

Parents teach children to ride a bike, hit a ball, tie a shoelace, and write their name, but many have never thought about teaching a child to pray. If your child learned to talk, then you can teach your child to pray. Why do I say that? Learning to pray is like learning to talk. Most children learned to talk by listening and then slowly beginning to say one word, then two, and eventually a sentence. "Say dada" is not only the way to teach a child to speak, but also the way to teach a child to pray.

When the disciples asked Jesus to teach them to pray, Jesus gave them the Lord's prayer rather than taught them the mechanics of praying. Teach your child to pray by praying together. Let your child hear your words and the passion of your heart. And do this again, and again, and again. A prayer-filled home is the best training ground to raise a praying child.

Ideas to teach children to pray:

◆ Memorize the Lord's Prayer together. Post it on the fridge so children see it daily or download the Lord's Prayer set to music and listen to it around the house.

◆ Read *What Every Child Should Know About Prayer* by Nancy Guthrie.

◆ Study the prayers of men and women in the Bible with your child, such as David's prayer of deliverance (Ps. 3), Hannah's prayer of praise (1 Sam. 2:1–10), David's prayer of repentance (Ps. 51), Solomon's prayer of dedication (1 Kings 8:22–61), and Paul's prayers for others (Eph.1:17–19; Eph. 3:16–19; Phil. 1:9–11; Col. 1:9–12).

◆ Teach your child how to pray Scripture. For example, if your child is feeling nervous, show them Proverbs 3:5–6 (NIV), "Trust in the Lord with all your heart and lean not on your own understanding; in all your ways acknowledge him, and he will make your paths straight." Then help your child to make each line into a prayer such as *Dear Jesus, I am feeling nervous right now! I am thinking about how things will turn out, and I'm afraid it might not go the way I want it to. Help me to trust you. Help me to remember that you have made my path straight. Please help me to rely on you, not just on my own thinking or skill. In Jesus' name, Amen.*

◆ Create a family prayer list. We went to an office store and purchased fun paper, cut thirty 4x6 rectangles, wrote the names of family, friends, missionaries, our pastor, the president, and others on a card, laminated, punched a hole in the corner and bound with a metal ring. We pray for one individual before dinner and flip to the next person the following night.

◆ Keep a family prayer journal. Intercede on behalf of others and record how God has answered prayers.

Describe your prayer life. Who and what do you pray for? Tell about a time that a prayer you prayed for your child was answered:

_____

_____

_____

Fully write out a passage of Scripture that you pray for your child:

_____

_____

_____

_____

_____

Who are the people you regularly pray for as a family? List their names here. Record prayers you saw God answer.

_____

_____

_____

Ask your child for prayer requests. Record those here. Pray together:

_____

_____

_____

Additional thoughts, observations, prayers, or memories:

_____

_____

_____

KNOWS THE GREAT HYMNS
OF THE FAITH

In a culture of ever-changing, newer-is-better approaches to music in the church, teaching your children traditional hymns becomes increasingly important. There is excellent contemporary Christian music as well, but often it takes less effort to teach children this music. Hymns require more intentionality, as they are often sung with less regularity. Hymns open the eyes and ears of young people to core doctrines, biblical lyrics, timeless musical melodies, and hymn writers, many of whom are heroes of the Christian faith. The following hymns are what we would consider a simple top-ten list. Feel free to add your own family favorites.

1. "A Mighty Fortress Is Our God," Martin Luther
2. "Amazing Grace," John Newton
3. "Be Thou My Vision," Dallan Forgaill
4. "Blessed Assurance," Fanny Crosby
5. "Come, Thou Fount of Every Blessing," Robert Robinson
6. "Doxology," Louis Bourgeois
7. "Great Is Thy Faithfulness," Thomas Chisholm/William M. Runyan

8. "Holy, Holy, Holy! Lord God Almighty," Reginald Heber/John B. Dykes
9. "How Great Thou Art," Carl Gustav Boberg
10. "How Deep the Father's Love for Us," Stuart Townend

Teaching hymns to your children:

Become familiar with the hymns, old and new, that you want your family to know. If you don't yet know the words or melodies, learn them alongside your children.

Find arrangements of the music that suit your family's style. Utilize music streaming apps to listen to multiple versions of the same song. Download and make them into a playlist. Listen to them often!

Teach a specific hymn correlating with a certain season. For example, teach "Jesus Paid It All" in the weeks leading up to Easter by playing and singing it with greater frequency.

Purchase a hymnal and use it. If you play an instrument, read the music. Use the printed lyrics to sing along with downloaded music.

Learn a hymn per week, month, or year—whatever time frame is comfortable for your family. Study the composer, the history of the time the hymn was written, scriptural parallels, and application for today.

If your church is more contemporary in its worship style, ask your pastor to incorporate hymns into the weekly Sunday gatherings.

Host or attend a hymn sing with friends and family.

Utilize books to make hymns come alive such as *Then Sings My Soul* by Robert J. Morgan, the Hymns for a Kid's Heart series by Bobbie Wolgemuth and Joni

Eareckson Tada, and the Great Hymns of Our Faith series by Joni Eareckson Tada, John MacArthur and Robert and Bobbie Wolgemuth.

Make a list of your personal favorite or special family hymns:

_____

_____

_____

_____

_____

Record the hymns you intentionally taught to your child. Include the date your child learned them and the season of life you chose to teach them.

_____

_____

_____

_____

_____

_____

_____

What were your child's favorite hymns and spiritual songs through the years?

Ages 0–5:

_____

_____

_____

Ages 6–10:

_____

_____

_____

Ages 11–14:

_____
_____
_____

Ages 15–18:

_____
_____
_____

Additional thoughts, observations, prayers, or memories:

_____
_____
_____
_____
_____
_____
_____
_____
_____
_____

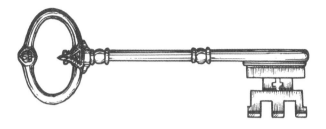

MEMORIZED KEY BIBLE VERSES

Bible memorization is foundational to spiritual growth. It's a way of filling our mind with what it needs in order to meditate on God's Word, triumph over temptation, be transformed into Christlikeness, and live in obedience to God. Memorizing Scripture is rewarding, strengthens one's prayer life, and improves our attitude and outlook on life. The good news is that children easily memorize information such as sports statistics or a new language, and we can leverage that for Scripture memorization. The Bible tells us to meditate daily on God's Word and to impress the truths of the Bible on the mind of our children. What better way to do that than by memorizing Scripture! The following is a simple list of recommended verses for children. Feel free to add your own favorites.

1. "In the beginning, God created the heavens and the earth" (Gen.1:1).
2. "Trust in the Lord with all your heart and do not lean on your own understanding" (Prov. 3:5).
3. "Children obey your parents in the Lord, for this is right" (Eph. 6:1).
4. "Love the Lord your God with all your heart and with all your soul and with all your strength" (Deut. 6:5).

5. "Do nothing out of selfish ambition, or vain conceit, but in humility consider others better than yourselves" (Phil. 2:3 NIV).

6. "Do everything without complaining or arguing" (Phil. 2:14 NIV).

7. "My dear brothers . . . Everyone should be quick to listen, slow to speak, and slow to become angry" (Jas. 1:19 NIV1984).

8. "For God so loved the world, that he gave his only Son, that whoever believes in him should not perish but have eternal life" (John 3:16).

9. "If you confess with your mouth that Jesus is Lord and believe in your heart that God raised him from the dead, you will be saved" (Rom. 10:9).

10. "For it is by grace you have been saved, through faith—and this is not from yourselves, it is the gift of God" (Eph. 2:8).

11. "Clothe yourselves with compassion, kindness, humility, gentleness and patience. Bear with each other and forgive one another if any of you has a grievance against someone. Forgive as the Lord forgave you. And over all these virtues put on love, which binds them all together in perfect unity" (Col. 3:12–14 NIV).

12. The Ten Commandments

13. The Lord's Prayer

Teaching bible memorization to your children

🔸 *Identify key verses for your child to memorize.* When our oldest was in preschool, Jen and I created a list of key verses we wanted our children to memorize and then had a graphic designer create an image for each verse to aid in memorization. We called it Rootworks: Hiding God's Word in Your Heart. A free download is available at GospelShapedFamily.com.

🔸 *Place key verses around your home in strategic locations.* As an example, we framed Joshua 24:15 ("As for me and my house we will serve the Lord") and placed it on the wall. We purchased a wooden piece of artwork with

Psalm 19:14 on it ("May the words of my mouth and the meditation of my heart be pleasing in your sight") and placed it on top of the piano.

Listen to Bible verses put to music. We created Roots Kids Worship for this purpose and we also love Seeds Family Worship. Our children learned the books of the Bible and the Ten Commandments through song.

Participate in Awana. One of the many strengths of Awana is helping children memorize Scripture in an age-appropriate, systematic way.

Make a list of Bible verses you would like your child to memorize and the date they learned them:

_____

_____

_____

Describe the fun and creative ways you helped your child memorize Bible verses.

_____

_____

_____

_____

_____

Additional thoughts, observations, prayers, or memories:

_____

_____

_____

PARTICIPATES IN WEEKLY CORPORATE WORSHIP

Gospel-centered, Bible-saturated corporate worship is supremely important for your family and children. The impact of hundreds of worship services with mom and dad during the child and teens years is extremely impactful. Let your children see you prioritize gathering for weekly worship over all other life options, sing to God with joy, give of your time and finances to the church, and submit to the preaching of the Word. Worshipping corporately is critical, as it will enable children to develop Christian fellowship, provide opportunities for serving, giving, missions, and engagement in discipleship ministries of the church.

In the Mulvihill family, it's a life milestone for a child to join the rest of the family for corporate worship. At age five or six, when a child has developed enough self-control to be in the worship service without disrupting others, he or she joins us for worship. If you can teach your child to eat at a table, you can train your child to worship corporately. The skills a child must learn to eat a physical meal are similar to the skills a child must learn to eat a spiritual meal. If your child is new to corporate worship, here are a few suggestions that may be helpful as you train the child:

Discuss worship expectations with your child. We tell our children that we expect them to be calm, quiet, and pay attention. Some of our children learned quickly. Others tested boundaries and needed loving guidance with a whisper in the ear, a squeeze on the thigh, or even an invitation to join a parent in the hallway to be reminded of expectations. If children are brand new to corporate worship, expect that quick learners will do well after a few weeks and slow learners will take a few months.

Provide tools not toys. We want children engaged, not occupied. It's great that children are present, but our goal is their participation. Rather than bringing cars or coloring books, bring a notebook, Bible, and pen. We encourage young children who cannot read to draw pictures of what they hear. Older children are expected to take notes and listen attentively. For accountability, we often have our children visit with the senior pastor after the service and show him their notes.

Teach your child the music you sing at church. We intentionally purchase and download songs that are sung during corporate worship at church and listen to them at home. We play worship music while children eat breakfast or clean, and in the process they become familiar with the melodies and lyrics. Guess what happens at church when they hear music they know and like? They sing! You can help your child by sitting in a child-friendly location so they can clearly see the front of the worship space.

Suckers! Our goal for children is busy hands and quiet mouths. When the pastor begins his sermon, we pass out a sucker to each of our children. The sucker usually helps a child pay attention for about ten minutes. We also strategically place the youngest children closest to a parent and the older ones at the end, with mom and dad sitting next to each other in the middle.

Say no to bathrooms and screens. We learned quickly that some children suddenly had to go to the bathroom and couldn't hold it during the sermon. We encourage children to go to the bathroom before the worship service and only give permission in rare instances. We initiated the "Are you going to wet your pants?" test to determine if the bathroom was necessary. We also do not allow screens during the service, unless it is to access the Bible or use an app to take notes. As parents, we try to set a good example by not texting, using social media, or checking email. Our children learn the value and form of worship by watching us. We want the affection of our heart and the focus of our mind to be on worshipping Christ, so we eliminate all distractions.

Ask questions on the ride home. Invite your children to share what they liked most about the sermon or a comment that stuck out to them. Sometimes our children will laugh about a funny story that was shared, and this is fine! It means they were listening. Other times, children will ask a clarifying question about what a word or concept means. This is an opportunity for you to see how your children are processing the sermon.

Resources to train your child for corporate worship:

◆ Read the article *The Family: Together in God's Presence* by John Piper.

◆ Read the book *Parenting in the Pew* by Robbie Castleman.

◆ Purchase a worship notebook or journal for your child to utilize during a worship service.

Describe church services at the church you attend. What is the name of your church? Where is it? What size is the congregation? Is the worship style traditional or contemporary? Where do you sit in the sanctuary? Who are the pastors? How long have you been members of the church? What do you love about your church?

_____

_____

_____

_____

_____

_____

Recall your own memories of attending church as a child. How are the church services you attend today similar or different?

_____

_____

_____

Describe in detail when your child began attending corporate worship. How old were they? What tools did you use to help your child engage with the sermon? What were your child's behaviors and observations? How did you celebrate this special milestone?

_____

_____

_____

Ask your child what his or her favorite songs are to sing in church. Record the answers here:

_____

_____

_____

Additional thoughts, observations, prayers, or memories:

_____

_____

_____

_____

_____

_____

CHAPTER 11

LIFE SKILLS

KNOWS HOW TO CARE FOR A PET

When I (Jen) was in first grade, our family adopted a tiny Siamese kitten named Cocoa. I loved Cocoa so much that I carried him around our house like a baby every minute I could. Thankfully, Cocoa liked being carried! Cocoa slept in my bed every night and was one of my greatest childhood treasures. He lived a long life for a cat and passed away when I was a sophomore in college. I learned many valuable life lessons by loving, caring for, and losing Cocoa. Pets make life richer; they become part of the family and are a tangible way for children to experience God's creation and what it means for us to "have dominion over the fish of the sea and over the birds of the heavens and over the livestock and over all the earth and over every creeping thing that creeps on the earth" (Gen. 1:26).

If your family doesn't own a pet, or if you don't have an affinity for animals, consider the long-term benefits of adding a pet to your family. Don't make an impulsive decision, as some pets can live as long as twenty years, but think seriously about whether you would like your child to experience growing up with a beloved family pet.

When teaching your child to care for a pet:

◆ Choose a pet that will fit your family lifestyle. If you live in a small apartment, a large dog probably isn't the best choice. If you have a phobia of reptiles, steer your child away from choosing a lizard or snake. Does anyone in your family have allergies? Take this into consideration before adopting a pet.

◆ Give your child responsibility for aspects of your pet's care. Small children are able to fill food and water bowls and brush a dog or cat. Elementary-age children are able to scoop out a litter box, take a dog to go potty in a backyard, and vacuum pet hair. Older kids can clean animal cages, walk dogs, and trim nails. Incorporate these tasks into your daily and weekly routines.

◆ Spend time together learning how to care for your pet. Our family adopted a puppy and we parents learned how to care for and train her along with the children. We read books about labradors together, attended puppy training classes, and spent countless hours walking her, teaching her to come, fetch, and sit. You can do the same with your child and pet, whether that pet is a large-breed dog or small hamster.

◆ Use the life and death of your pet as a gateway to deeper conversation. Did your child forget to feed the rabbit? Discuss how it feels to be hungry and without food. Is your cat going to have kittens? Watch the birth. Allow your child to make connections and ask questions about their own birth. Is your pet near the end of his or her life? Share the hope of the Gospel with your child.

Describe our family pets. What are their names? What kind of animal are they? What color are they? How did you acquire them? What are their mannerisms?

_____

_____

_____

List the ways your child works to take care of your pets:

_____

_____

_____

Record a funny or memorable moment with your family pets:

_____

_____

_____

Take a photo of your child with his or her pet. Keep a copy here:

Additional thoughts, observations, prayers, or memories:

_____

_____

_____

_____

_____

_____

UNDERSTANDS HOW TO NAVIGATE THE INTERNET AND SOCIAL MEDIA

I remember when the internet arrived at my house. I was in ninth grade. I got my first email address in college. I joined my first social media site in my mid twenties. Much has changed since these early days, but one thing remains constant: We cannot escape it. The internet and social media are not going away, and we cannot become digital hermits. We need to teach our children how to navigate technology, explain to them the value and the dangers, train them to use it as we would any tool, and show them how to be techwise and digitally self-controlled.

The internet and social media are useful, like guns and painkillers and fire and razor-sharp knives—and lots of other things that can ruin our life. I'm grateful for knives. I use one every day, but I would never give one to my child without careful oversight nor would I hand my child a gun without proper training. The same is true for internet and social media usage. Here are a few things we have learned with our children:

◈ Think about your motive and purpose for your child's social media and internet usage. Help your child answer why they are on social media. What purpose does it serve in their life? What is a child gaining from technology use?

What pitfalls need to be protected against? Technology should serve us, not enslave us. It should help build relationships, not harm them. It exists as a means to fulfill the Great Commission and the Great Commandment, not to build our own kingdom or name.

◆ Recognize that screens are as addictive as any drug, go right to the pleasure center of the brain, and impact brain function. Research the impact of screens on children and make an informed decision about what place technology has in your home. Read the online articles "Fighting the Internet Invasion of Childhood" by Martin Kutnowski and "A Silicon Valley School that Doesn't Compute" by Matt Richtel.

◆ Don't be afraid to say no to media. Screen time makes children moody, bored, and lazy. Their minds become over-entertained so that real life seems dull. Boredom dies away as media usage goes down. Screens make children depressed and unmotivated, and they reduce physical activity levels. We prioritize time outdoors and surround our children with good books. We also try (not always successfully) to limit screen usage to the weekend, special occasions, or remove it entirely for weeks at a time. Our grade school-aged children are limited to one hour of video games a week, and we have tech-free weeks during the year that are a blessing to our family.

◆ Delay giving children devices until they are truly needed. In our home, we do not allow our children to own a smartphone or tablet of their own due to the impact of screens and danger of pornography. Our high school-aged son has an iPod that allows him to text with friends, call us, and listen to music. We disabled the internet on it and put a parental restriction that requires approval for all app downloads until he is older, and we restrict usage to only the living room or kitchen. We would never allow our children to enter a room full of pornographic videos, yet parents think nothing of handing their child a smartphone with unlimited access to porn. Will people think you are weird and a control freak? Probably, but what's more important—what others think of you or the health of your child?

♦ Gradually give older children more freedoms, under the watchful eye of parents. Greater freedoms should be granted when maturity and responsibility are displayed. A goal to consider: A child should be able to handle the internet before leaving the home, as they will need to have the discernment and fortitude to navigate the pressures and temptations of the internet on their own. Recognize that allowing greater freedom does not mean that you are hands-off. There are tools and apps that allow you to see what children are doing online, monitor time usage, and place boundaries on technology use.

♦ Talk about online dangers such as pornography, bullying, scams, and stalkers. Recognize that the internet is the playground while the heart is the battleground. What happens on a screen is an extension of what is happening in the heart, so help your children to guard their heart and mind as well as to be wise and discerning online.

♦ Do not give a child unmonitored, unrestricted access to the internet. If porn enters the picture, take decisive action cutting off access. The moral and spiritual damage from porn is serious, so fight porn in your family with everything you've got. Put internet filters and accountability tools in place to help a child succeed.

♦ Provide instruction about wise social media usage. Consider topics such as sharing too much information, how posts may impact future employment, the permanence of social media posts even after being deleted, how to use privacy and location settings, not friending strangers, nonnegotiable parental supervision,- self-worth issues, and how biblical principles for speech and the way we treat others should guide our online behavior. Discuss how social media offers a glimpse into the lives of others, but only a distorted snapshot. Children need to be taught not to define their worth by the number of likes but by the standards of Scripture.

♦ Be prepared for failures. Think ahead. What will the consequences be? Be mindful of your response, as your child may remember it his or her entire life. Lead with grace.

For older children who have been given too much freedom on technology, consider a detox. You may need to hit the refresh button and establish new boundaries and guidelines. When new boundaries are placed on technology, be prepared to answer your child's questions. Parents need to model healthy online behavior, so new technology expectations should apply to you as well.

Consider reading the books *The Tech-Wise Family* by Andy Crouch and *12 Ways Your Phone is Changing You* by Tony Reinke.

List online and social media guidelines for your family. Be as detailed as possible. Include what is acceptable based upon your child's age. What devices and social media platforms are allowed? What sorts of daily time limits are enforced?

_____

_____

_____

Describe your child's media consumption at ages five, ten, fifteen and eighteen. How much screen time does your child get per day? What platforms and websites do they visit frequently? Evaluate what is working well and what changes need to be made:

_____

_____

_____

Additional thoughts, observations, prayers, or memories:

_____

_____

_____

KNOWS HOW TO
COMMUNICATE WELL

A child who can speak confidently, clearly, and concisely can go just about any-where and do just about anything. If your child learns how to speak well, they will be light-years ahead of peers and it will set them apart from others. Public speaking and communicating effectively are learnable skills and two of the most valuable for your child to master.

Many young adults do not communicate well. They have poor grammar, mumble, or cannot articulate an idea clearly or effectively. Many rely on emotional arguments and utilize ad hominem attacks or a logical fallacy to get their point across. The fear of public speaking affects nearly seventy-five percent of all people and causes anxiety or an inability to speak clearly. Many individuals struggle to communicate emotions and empathy with friends and family. The ability to think critically, speak articulately, communicate confi-dently, and persuade others with the spoken word is a skill that will benefit your child in immeasurable ways.

3 Ways to improve public speaking skills:

◈ *Read.* Reading teaches good grammar, expands vocabulary and critical think-ing, and provides examples of logical arguments.

◆ *Write*. One way to learn to speak well is to write, which clarifies thoughts. Reading leads to creativity. Writing leads to clarity.

◆ *Practice*. Look for opportunities for public speaking, such as in front of family. Anxiety and fear decrease with preparation and practice.

12 ways to strengthen interpersonal communication skills:

Study these twelve passages with your child and discuss the communication principle in each verse. Ask your child which areas they struggle with.

◆ "Everyone should be quick to listen, slow to speak, and slow to become angry" (Jas. 1:19).

◆ "Do not let any unwholesome talk come out of your mouths, but only what is helpful for building others up according to their needs, that it may benefit those who listen" (Eph. 4:29 NIV).

◆ "Fools find no pleasure in understanding but delight in airing their own opinions" (Prov. 18:2 NIV).

◆ "The words of the reckless pierce like swords, but the tongue of the wise brings healing" (Prov. 12:18 NIV).

◆ "But now you must rid yourselves of all such things as these: rage, anger, malice, slander, and filthy language from your lips" (Col. 3:8 NIV).

◆ "May the words of my mouth and the meditations of my heart be pleasing in your sight, O Lord" (Ps. 19:14 NIV).

◆ "The heart of the righteous weighs its answers, but the mouth of the wicked gushes evil" (Prov. 15:28 NIV).

◆ "A gentle answer turns away wrath, but a harsh word stirs up anger" (Prov. 15:1).

◆ "Do not repay evil with evil or insult with insult. On the contrary, repay evil with blessing" (1 Pet. 3:9 NIV).

◆ "Those who guard their mouths and their tongues keep themselves from calamity" (Prov. 21:23 NIV).

◆ "Gracious words are a honeycomb, sweet to the soul and healing to the bones" (Prov. 16:24 NIV).

◆ "It is to one's honor to avoid strife, but every fool is quick to quarrel" (Prov. 20:3 NIV).

Communication skills checklist:

◆ Can your child form an argument that is logical, concise, and clear?

◆ Can your child speak with empathy, self-control, and respect for others?

◆ Has your child learned to speak words that are gracious and gentle rather than harsh or hurtful?

◆ Has your child learned to be quick to listen and slow to become angry?

◆ Does your child know how to have a conversation with people of all ages? Can your child hold a conversation with someone who is decades older or younger than they are?

◆ Can your child listen attentively to understand another person's point of view?

◆ Has your child learned to ask questions to gain clarity or carry a conversation?

◆ Does your child pay attention to nonverbal communication such as body language, tone, posture, facial expressions, and eye contact?

◆ Can your child tell a compelling story?

Review the communication skills checklist above. What skills has your child mastered? What skills do you need to teach?

_____

_____

_____

What activities or opportunities did you facilitate to help your child learn to communicate well?

_____

_____

_____

Additional thoughts, observations, prayers, or memories:

_____

_____

_____

_____

_____

_____

_____

_____

_____

_____

DEVELOPED AN
APPRECIATION FOR NATURE

When we were unloading the truck during the move to our small hobby farm, it didn't take long to have our first experience in nature. Within minutes, one of the children was running across the yard at a full sprint, screaming at the top of his lungs. A cloud of bees followed him. He had accidentally discovered a hive in the ground and the bees won the battle that day. Before he even knew what was happening, he had already been stung a dozen times. Today, we're hobby beekeepers, and a sting is a badge of honor.

It took a while for our children to enjoy being outside. Now we can't keep them inside. But it wasn't always that way. What did we do to nurture a love for nature in our children? We send our children outside just about every day, no matter the weather. We have a saying in Minnesota, "There's no bad weather. There are just the wrong clothes." Bad or cold weather isn't an excuse to stay inside. Some parents will say, "But my children stand at the door and cry or complain." Our children did that for a few weeks too, but that didn't last long once they discovered the joy of being outside.

We did a crazy thing that solidified a love of nature for our children. We got rid of the video game system. There were tears. Our sons grieved as if their most beloved family member had died. We felt like horrible parents. But that only lasted for a short season before we started to see the benefits, so we also removed the television from a central location in our home. What do our children do with all the extra time they gained from not playing video games or watching much TV? They go outside. They play in the woods, build a fort, make a bonfire, shoot a pellet gun, pick flowers, swing on swings, tend to animals, explore a creek, go sledding, dig in the dirt, climb trees, cut firewood, or throw a ball. If our children don't need a bath every night, then they aren't playing hard enough. We believe that children need to be dirty, sweaty, and tired at the end of every day. That's a good day!

Children today don't know how to play. The joy of play, the value of being active, the beauty of being in God's great outdoors is exchanged for sitting for long hours, listening, and for seeing an image on the screen. We wonder, why is Jon hyper? Why are Emily's eyes glazed over? Why don't they have any interest in learning? In today's society, we sedate them with medication, put them in front of a screen, and tell them to sit quiet and still. Children need to play, and move, and be outdoors. A must-read book is *The Last Child in the Woods*, which coins the term "Nature Deficit Disorder" and explains how an obsession with being indoors and electronic media, combined with parental fears of the outdoors and relinquishment of being in nature, are connected with depression, obesity, and disorders in children.

There are common factors that encourage play: space, lots of time, being outdoors, the freedom to make noise and get dirty. We need to have the margin in our schedule to allow for these. Children's lives are over-scheduled and—however valuable each activity is—this has eliminated the space and time children need to play. Access to nature is essential to healthy development. Children who experience nature do better academically. Children who spend more time outside pay more attention inside. They develop an awe and appreciation for the wonders of God's creation. So turn off the screen and get your children outside!

Does your family have outdoor places that are special to you? List them here. Where are they? Why are they special? What memories have you made in those places?

_____

_____

_____

Ask your child what is their favorite season of the year and why. Record their answer here:

_____

_____

_____

What activities does your child enjoy doing outdoors? If your child does not appreciate nature and being outdoors, what can you do to foster appreciation of the outdoors in them?

_____

_____

_____

Additional thoughts, observations, prayers, or memories:

_____

_____

_____

_____

_____

_____

_____

_____

_____

_____

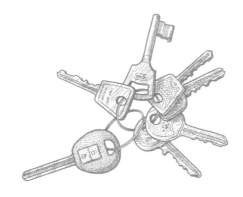

KNOWS HOW TO RESPONSIBLY DRIVE AND MAINTAIN A CAR

Training a new driver comes with its share of wide eyes, white knuckles, and maybe even a few fender benders. But getting a driver's license is an important rite of passage into adulthood. If this stage of life is a way off for you, then it will be helpful to know what to expect and to plan for this season before it comes. Here are a few suggestions to help you navigate this season when it arrives:

- Model good driving habits. Once a child is interested in learning to drive, they will pay attention to how you drive and handle yourself on the road.

- Expect that your child will become critical of your driving. In their eyes, your years of driving experience will evaporate and every one of your bad driving habits will be examined and discussed to prove your lack of knowledge and driving ability.

- One parent will be better at training a child to drive than the other. In our home, that is Jen. Her combination of patience, positivity, and graciousness is a great fit for this task.

- Think about a strategy for music, friends, and car expenses. Save yourself conflict and make a plan for music usage while driving, for when friends can ride in the car, and for how car expenses such as gas, insurance, repairs, and ownership will be handled. Music and friends can cause distracted driving, so apply caution in these areas. Have your child assume some of the financial responsibilities so there is ownership and accountability.

◆ Every child approaches driving differently. Every child learns differently and has a different timeline for when and how they get their driver's license. Tailor your teaching to the needs of your child and be flexible!

◆ Riding lawn mowers and four-wheelers provide good practice for younger children. While nothing will replicate driving on a road with other cars, learning the basics of paying attention, using their senses, and being responsible in general is helpful. Good, basic driving skills never go to waste.

◆ Don't skimp on driving hours. Require that your child practice with you in all weather conditions. The ability to drive safely in the rain, snow, or dark is a learned skill.

◆ Teach your child basic car maintenance. Show your child how to change the oil, replace a flat tire, and jump a dead battery. If you are mechanical, invite your child to join you when you are working on your car. If something sounds wrong or a warning light comes on, remind your child not to ignore it.

◆ Talk about responsibility and safety. We follow driving laws, are courteous to other drivers, wear a seatbelt at all times, and ensure the safety of passengers and other drivers by keeping all body parts in the vehicle and not exceeding speed limits.

Describe in detail the vehicle your child will use to learn to drive. Is it old or new? What color is it? How did you acquire it?

_____

_____

_____

_____

Record memories of teaching your child to drive. Was your child excited or nervous? A slow or fast driver? What situations were funny, nerve-racking, or dangerous?

_____

_____

_____

Tell about the day your child passed his or her driver's exam. What was the date? Where did he or she take the test? Where did your child go on his or her first solo drive? How did you celebrate? Take a photo of your child with their new driver's license. Keep a copy here:

_____

_____

_____

_____

_____

_____

List your family's rules and guidelines for new drivers:

_____

_____

_____

_____

_____

Additional thoughts, observations, prayers, or memories:

_____

_____

_____

_____

_____

_____

_____

_____

_____

_____

_____

CHAPTER 12

RELATIONAL SKILLS

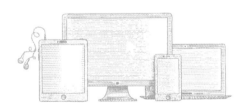

CONFIDENT IN
MAKING INTRODUCTIONS

L ydia arrived for her interview ten minutes late, but at least she apologized and had a smile on her face. I was interviewing for a ministry position at the church I pastored, and Lydia was one of three individuals being considered for the position. Being late to our meeting didn't help, but that was only the beginning of Lydia's bad first impression. Her shirt had a stain, and she was dressed so casually that she could have been mistaken for a fitness instructor. When I held out my hand to welcome Lydia, what happened was more of a finger shake than a handshake. Before the interview even began, Lydia already had multiple strikes against her. Unsurprisingly, she didn't get the job.

A good introduction is priceless, and as Lydia's case reveals, it doesn't come naturally for everyone. It only takes a moment to establish a strong or weak first impression. Whether we want to admit it or not, first impressions impact future opportunities and influence how people interact with us. A good introduction could be the first step to an open door, a new relationship, or a significant partnership. Parents do their child a great service by showing them how to confidently introduce themselves. Here are some things to consider teaching your child.

Tips to confidently introduce oneself:

◆ *Dress for the occasion.* The biggest factor that affects others' first impression is physical appearance. Children need to be taught to take the extra time to shower, style their hair, ensure their clothes are clean and fit properly, and are appropriate for the occasion. For special occasions such as interviews, they should pick an outfit they feel confident in and practice wearing it around home so there are no wardrobe malfunctions.

◆ *Address others by name.* Everyone loves to hear their own name. It places the focus on them and tells them they matter. If your child is unsure how to address someone, they should ask them what they would like to be called. When in doubt, they should choose the more formal option such as Mr., Mrs. or Dr.

◆ *Smile.* Everyone loves a smile—just make sure it's sincere. One research study found that 48 percent of individuals identified a smile as the most memorable feature they recall when meeting someone for the first time.[6]

◆ *Make eye contact.* Making eye contact is a way of showing respect and communicates that we are interested in what someone has to say. Looking down communicates a lack of confidence, and looking past someone communicates that we are uninterested. If a child is shy and struggles to maintain eye contact, this is an important skill to practice.

◆ *Give a firm handshake.* A strong handshake makes a strong impression, while a weak handshake makes a weak impression. For a strong handshake, extend the thumb as far away from the pointer finger as possible, aim for web to web, and do not squeeze too hard or hold onto someone's hand too long.

◆ *Do your homework.* If your child is making an introduction for career reasons, encourage him or her to research all they can about the person or organization and learn about mission, goals, and accomplishments. People love it when others know something about them, and this provides talking points during the conversation.

Be aware of your body language. Be mindful of yawning, crossing arms, or slouching, as any of these may be interpreted as a sign of disinterest. Use nonverbals to show interest such as nods, smiles, and short expressions of agreement.

Practice! Practice is what helps develop confidence. Have your child rehearse scenarios, practice at home, practice at church, and practice in other social settings. The more one practices, the more natural it will become. Home is a great place to start.

Share a memory of a time when you practiced or discussed each of the following with your child. What was the occasion? Record the date and any other details you'd like to remember:

Dressing for the occasion:

_____

_____

_____

Addressing others by name:

_____

_____

_____

Intentionally smiling:

_____

_____

_____

Making eye contact:

_____

_____

_____

Giving a firm handshake:

_____

_____

_____

Doing your homework:

_____

_____

_____

Being aware of your body language:

_____

_____

_____

Additional thoughts, observations, prayers, or memories:

_____

_____

_____

_____

_____

_____

LEARNED HOW TO DEVELOP
AND MAINTAIN A FRIENDSHIP

Friends are wonderful. They provide some of the greatest joys and most memorable moments in life. They also can lead to some of the greatest hurts in life. A great friend is a precious gift from God. The Bible tells us, "A sweet friendship refreshes the soul" (Prov. 27:9). One of the most common laments from parents I heard as a pastor was that their child did not have a close friend. Likewise, many men and women struggle to develop deep and lasting friendships in adulthood. You are giving your child an amazing gift if you help him or her learn how to develop and maintain friendships. Here are four suggestions we've learned as parents.

The first thing we've learned is to prioritize the church as the center of relationships that all life revolves around. Peer groups are extremely influential for young people, especially as they move into the teenage years. Children tend to become friends with those they spend the most time with, which is why it becomes important to make the commitment to attend church weekly and become actively involved in church life. If family life revolves around athletics or academics, friendships will form with individuals in these locations. We've seen it happen time after time: If children do not have close friends at church, they begin attending less and less until they stop attending all together. Your child needs a Christ-centered community, and by God's design that is the family and the church.

The second thing we've learned is that the family is the training ground for how to develop and maintain healthy relationships. The interactions, characteristics, and state of the relationships in our home between the parents, between parent and child, and between one sibling and another teaches children the relational behaviors they will carry with them into adulthood. We have found that the "one another" commands of the Bible are helpful to study as a family. Two of our favorite passages to read and discuss with our children are Colossians 3:12–14 and Philippians 2:3–5, which provide biblical principles that guide our interactions with one another. Children need to learn how to biblically navigate conflict in relationships, so focus significant energy in this area. While there will be no perfect relationships until heaven, the Bible provides hope that our relationships can be characterized by gentleness, compassion, forgiveness, patience, honesty, and love. God's grace makes this possible, even for flawed people living in a broken world.

The third priority we've had with our children is to train them to identify godly characteristics in potential friends. Proverbs provides many negative characteristics to avoid and positive traits to pursue in our relationships with others. Study Proverbs together, identifying the verses that address relationships, and help your child apply them to their choice of friends. We teach our children to identify godly individuals they enjoy being around and to initiate a friendship rather than to passively wait for an invitation. One way we have helped our children is to let them know that our home is always open, their friends are always welcome, and food is always available. We provide regular opportunities through father-son campouts at our home, flag football in our yard, fantasy football with friends, Christmas baking parties, sledding in the yard, ringing the Salvation Army bell together at Christmas, and even work days on our home spent together with friends. Combine time together with the same friends at church and at home and there is a high likelihood that deep, genuine friendships will form.

The fourth principle we teach, and maybe the most important, is that healthy relationships with others are only possible when we love God first. Loving God helps us love others well. God shows us how to love others by how he loves us, ultimately displayed by Jesus on the cross. The Gospel is our map and mirror for how to maintain healthy relationships. The same measure of grace and forgiveness we have been given by God is to be extended by us to others. C.S. Lewis said it best: "When I have learnt to love God better than my earthly dearest, I shall love my earthly dearest better than I do now. In so far as I learn to love my earthly dearest at the expense of God and *instead* of God, I shall be moving towards the state in which I shall not love my earthly dearest at all. When first things are put first, second things are not suppressed but increased."[7]

Does your child have siblings? Ask your child what he or she likes most about each of them. Write their answers here:

_____

_____

_____

If your child has good friends, who are they? Record their names and how your child met them:

_____

_____

Tell about a special memory your child had with a friend:

_____

_____

Who were your best friends growing up? Are they still your friends today? What wisdom would you share with your child about choosing lifelong friendships?

_____

_____

Additional thoughts, observations, prayers, or memories:

_____

_____

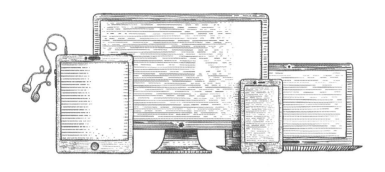

KNOWS PHONE, TEXT, AND EMAIL ETIQUETTE

A boss once told me, "If you can communicate well, you'll never have trouble getting a job or maintaining relationships." That's proven true so far in life. Phone calls, texts, and emails are a big part of the communication landscape, and skilled communicators have learned to utilize these tools. Children will benefit from learning which to use under different circumstances and basic etiquette for each form of digital communication. While there are no hard-and-fast rules, here are nine norms that should be considered. Add your own thoughts to the list!

Nine important digital communication skills to learn:

💎 ***Communicate clearly.*** The receiver should not be confused about what we are trying to say. Make sure the message cannot be misinterpreted. Pay attention to abbreviations and emojis.

💎 ***Respond within 24 hours.*** If someone spoke to us in person, it would be considered rude to ignore them and not respond. The same goes for calls, texts, and emails. Be as prompt as possible. Responsiveness is a basic skill to learn in life and will strengthen relationships and provide good customer service. If we cannot respond promptly, offer an apology.

Keep it short. Get to the point. Omit unnecessary information.

Reread and edit. Your communication is a reflection of the quality of your work. Catch and correct errors in spelling and grammar.

Expect that anything said by email will be public knowledge. If a child has sensitive information to share, don't send it by text or email; talk by phone or in person.

Use reply all and group texts sparingly. Don't send a message to everyone if it only needs to be read by one or two people.

Refrain from emotional responses. Hasty emotional responses typically result in regret and hurt relationships. If something makes us angry, sad, or anxious, then delay responding until the next day. Prioritize phone calls and in-person conversations when emotions are involved.

Practice using the telephone. Give your child the task of making phone calls to inquire about products at a store, to make a doctor appointment, or chat with a friend. Coach them on what questions to ask, how to write down essential details, and how to ask questions to spur conversation.

Learn which form of communication to use. Texts, emails, and phone calls all serve different purposes. Texts are great for short, informal messages and are best utilized with family, friends, and coworkers. Emails are ideal for a detailed message, when urgency of a response is not a factor, and for different time zones. Phone calls are good for lengthy topics or sensitive subjects.

Below, record the telephone, texting and email skills you taught your child and the date he or she learned them.

Email skills: signatures, out-of-office messages, spell check, full sentences, salutations, responsiveness, and more.

_____

_____

_____

Text skills: brevity, abbreviations, emojis, responsiveness, and important texting norms.

_____

_____

_____

Phone skills: proper greetings, voicemails, and essential phone etiquette.

_____

_____

_____

Additional thoughts, observations, prayers, or memories:

_____

_____

_____

_____

_____

KNOWS WHY AND WHOM TO DATE

Your child needs clarity about why to date and whom they should pursue for marriage. Many individuals have regrets about their dating days, and if the divorce rate is any indication, many had a difficult time choosing the right person to marry. What is the purpose of dating? Date to find your mate. Use dating as the discerning process for marriage. The goal of dating is clarity. Its intention is marriage. Its danger is intimacy. Its requirement is being equally yoked. God's design for marriage speaks to the design for dating. We want to caution our children against entering into a dating relationship casually, carelessly, or quickly. Dating doesn't exist to provide a young person with someone to hang out with or make out with. Almost always, these dating arrangements leave somebody wounded. It's good to remind our children that their hearts weren't built to be borrowed.

Biblical guidelines for choosing a date:

◆ *Avoid early dating.* The Song of Songs encourages readers to refrain from pursuing romantic love until the time is right. Three times we are reminded "not to awaken love" until the right time (Song 2:7; 3:5; 8:4). It is important to recognize that if there is a right time, then there is also a wrong time to enter into a romantic relationship. The word *awaken* literally means to arouse, stimulate, and stir. Solomon warns us not to intentionally stimulate or arouse love until it can be acted on.

🔷 **Only date a committed Christian.** The Bible is clear that a Christian is to marry only another Christian: "Do not be yoked together with unbelievers" (2 Cor. 6:14 NIV).

🔷 **Remember the God-designed roles of husband and wife.** Our children should take God's principles for marriage and backtrack them into the dating relationship as criteria to discern whom to pursue.

🔷 **Avoid dating an individual with habitually negative character traits.** The Bible, especially in the book of Proverbs, spends quite a bit of time telling young people whom to avoid, such as gossips, slanderers, and those who are angry. Parents are wise to apply this instruction to the dating process.

🔷 **Identify who is to be desired as a spouse.** Search the Scriptures to know God's guidelines for godly relationships and what He requires in a spouse. The book of Proverbs is helpful for this task.

🔷 **Take red flags seriously.** Warning signs should not be discounted as insignificant. Red flags to take seriously include addiction, abuse, deception, workaholism, unfaithfulness, and narcissistic tendencies.

🔷 **Choose your date carefully.** Eventually, one of your child's dates will be his or her mate. This should lead to a selective dating process. If a person isn't marriageable, then he or she isn't datable.

🔷 **Know when to say yes.** If God's criteria are met, your child is free to date and marry whomever he or she wishes. God's guidelines are meant to be freeing.

They clearly reveal who is in bounds and who is out of bounds for marriage. The young person who obeys the Lord and seeks a future mate according to God's standards will experience what Proverbs 18:22 describes: "He who finds a good wife [or husband] finds a good thing and obtains favor from the Lord."

What dating guidelines have you established for our family? List them here.

_____

_____

_____

What wisdom or important principles have you taught your child about dating?

_____

_____

_____

Record observations and memories of your child's dating years:

_____

_____

_____

Additional thoughts, observations, prayers, or memories:

_____

_____

_____

_____

_____

PREPARED FOR
MARRIAGE AND SEX

A child will make few decisions more important than whom they marry. Children of all ages need to be taught the meaning of marriage and the role of husband and wife, as well as what to look for in a future spouse. The biblical guidance for all parents to remember: *Go where the Bible goes.* You can be confident and comfortable talking about subjects with your child that God addresses with children in the Bible.

The pattern of Scripture is to teach children God's truths regarding marriage, sex, and purity. In Joshua 8:35 we observe children participating with the entire community of Israel as they heard the first five books of the Bible read out loud, which means we can directly observe key passages about marriage such as Genesis 2:24–25 being taught to children—both young and old.

In Ephesians 6:4 children are directly commanded to obey their parents. For a young person to hear, "Children, obey your parents," he or she had to be present, sitting with the rest of the congregation, listening to the entirety of Ephesians being read. Along with the rest of the congregation, children were taught the biblical role of husband and wife in marriage as well as the meaning and purpose of marriage (Eph. 5:22–33).

Here are six biblical truths every child must know about marriage:

◆ *Marriage is created by God.* God designed marriage, therefore God gets to define marriage. Marriage is one man and one woman for life.

◆ *Marriage is for God's glory.* God created marriage and has a purpose for it.

◆ *Marriage is good.* Enthusiastically champion marriage to your child.

◆ *Marriage is the expected norm.* It is not good for man to be alone, unless gifted for singleness.

◆ *Marriage is a covenant.* It is a make-it-and-never-break-it promise.

◆ *Marriage is the context for children.* God commands married couples to be fruitful and multiply. Your child needs a biblical vision for having and raising godly children.

The pattern of Scripture is for parents to talk with children about the meaning of marriage, the biblical role of husband and wife, the purpose of sex, sexual purity, adultery, homosexuality, and divorce. Parents have no need to be unsure about the content they should discuss with their children. Just follow God's lead. Cover the topics He covers with children. Parents have the critical job of articulating and embodying a biblical vision of marriage to their children.

We live in a sex-saturated culture that provides 24/7 access to our children through the media and an educational system that teaches unbiblical views about marriage and gender—that necessitates early and regular conversations with our children. Major exposure to sexual content and erroneous views of marriage occurs for many children in the early grade school years.

The time to begin addressing marriage isn't the teens or early adult years. Ideally, the teen years are the time to put the finishing touches on a long and lengthy conversation that has been happening since children were young. How can parents talk about this subject with children? Here are five suggestions to utilize:

- **The experiences you have.** Jen and I purposefully bring our children to weddings, which creates an opportunity to talk about God's design for marriage.

- **The shows you watch.** What does your child see on TV or in movies that invites discussion or can be used intentionally? For example, if your kids watch Disney princess movies, there are plenty of opportunities to talk about marriage.

- **The books you read.** We had great discussions with our children about marriage when we read the Little House on the Prairie series and Laura married Almonzo and in the Penderwicks series when the children's father was widowed.

- **The toys children play with.** Barbies and dolls are great discussion starters for girls.

- **The Scriptures you read.** As you read through the Bible with children, discuss the passages that address marriage, dating, and purity.

The opportunities to talk about marriage, dating, and purity occur often with children. Your job is to recognize opportunities and intentionally capitalize on them. Preparation for marriage can begin today as you teach your child biblical principles about marriage, pray for your child's future spouse, and help your child protect his or her heart from sexual immorality. For additional help, read *Preparing Children for Marriage: How to Teach God's Good Design for Marriage, Sex, Purity, and Dating*. You will find seventeen Bible studies to have with your child on these topics in the book.

How has a godly marriage been modeled to your child?

Share a memory of attending a wedding with your child. Whose wedding was it? What observations or questions did your child have?

_____
_____
_____

If you are married, describe your wedding for your child. Where were you married? Who was there? What was the weather like that day? Who was the officiating pastor? What food was served? Provide as much detail as possible:

_____
_____
_____

Has your child experienced the pain of divorce? How has divorce impacted your child's life or the lives of people close to them? Give your child the opportunity to ask questions, process, and mourn. Record your child's experiences and how you have helped them navigate divorce:

_____
_____
_____

Additional thoughts, observations, prayers, or memories:

_____
_____
_____
_____
_____

Therefore a man shall leave his father
and his mother and hold fast to his wife,
and they shall become one flesh.
And the man and his wife were both
naked and were not ashamed.

Genesis 2:24-25

CHAPTER 13

WORK AND MONEY MANAGEMENT

EXHIBITS A
STRONG WORK ETHIC

Jen and I have been renovating a one-hundred-year-old farm house and we needed a concrete sidewalk removed and a refrigerator carried into our home, two difficult jobs that required hard work and heavy lifting. We hired Daniel, a college student who had just launched a new business called His Workmanship, to get the jobs done. Daniel and his co-worker arrived at our home with jackhammers, a huge trailer, and a can-do attitude. Daniel exhibited the work ethic every parent wants for a child. He was kind, respectful, on time, hardworking, and did an excellent job. Daniel even offered to take ten percent off our bill if we read him John 3:16, which was printed at the bottom of the invoice. Daniel's work ethic combined with his understanding of work as a sphere of ministry to exercise dominion over creation is an example for parents to replicate with their children.

In today's world, children need to overcome the temptations of laziness, apathy, and entitlement to mature into a godly adult. Children naturally gravitate to either work avoidance or workaholism, so parents need to be intentional to help a child develop a biblical work ethic. Children learn to work hard through opportunity and example. Daily chores are a great way to begin, progressing to small paying jobs, a commitment to do one's best in schoolwork, volunteer opportunities, and part-time work all help children develop a strong work ethic. The Bible teaches us how to approach work: "Whatever you do, work at it with all your heart, as working for the Lord, not for human masters, since you know that you will receive an inheritance from the Lord as a reward. It is the Lord Christ you are serving" (Col. 3:23–24 NIV).

God created work and called it good. He gave Adam and Eve work to do by naming animals, caring for the garden, and having children. When sin entered the world, all things, including work, came under a curse, and our toil is now marked by struggle and sweat. Work is an opportunity to glorify God, a way to love our neighbor and to reorder the natural world to be in harmony with God's original design. Many Christians live with a disconnected relationship between work and God. For many people, work either exists as a means to pay bills, as a way to define ourselves, or as a secular area of life separated from God. In work, we exercise our God-given governance of a small part of the world. Work is the God-ordained means of exercising dominion over the earth in both stewardship and in restoring that which is broken—whether it's the living room, classroom, or boardroom. Our work is also a God-designed means of having purpose, loving God, and serving others.

Consider the following ideas to train your child to develop a strong work ethic:

- *Begin early.* One of our mottos is "don't do for a child what a child can do for themselves." Give young children simple tasks that increase with age and ability.

- *Encourage children to do a complete job.* Train your children to do excellent work and not cut corners or settle for mediocre work.

- *Teach children the twin enemies of good work:* procrastination and perfectionism.

- *Learn perseverance.* Children need to learn that when things get difficult, they don't give up or quit. Let children struggle and fail forward rather than completing the task for them or telling them they don't have to do it.

◆ *Teach entrepreneurial skills.* Teach children to monetize their talents, skills, or passions. Learning to work for someone is important, but learning ways to supplement income or start a business is essential in today's world. We've encouraged our children to learn a single trade before graduating from high school. Purchase the .com of your child's first and last name to retain for his or her future use.

◆ *Work with your children.* When possible, include your children in home-improvement projects, vehicle maintenance, and yard work.

◆ *Take your children with you when you serve.* Work associated with serving builds character and is enjoyable. We serve regularly as a family in children's ministry, as greeters at our church, in leading worship, and a child gets to be my ministry associate when I travel to speak at a church.

◆ *Make chores a responsibility for all family members.* Chores are the training ground to learn to work hard with joy and excellence.

◆ *Utilize the following books to gain a vision for work as a sphere of ministry. God's Pleasure at Work* by Dr. Christian Overman, *Created for Work* by Bob Schultz, and *Adorning the Dark* by Andrew Peterson help older children understand how to live out the creation mandate (Gen. 1:28) through their future vocation or calling in life.

What responsibilities have you given your child to help them learn a strong work ethic?

_____

_____

_____

_____

_____

"For Christians to influence the world with the truth of God's Word requires the recovery of the great Reformation doctrine of vocation...The church needs to cultivate Christian artists, musicians, novelists, filmmakers, journalists, attorneys, teachers, scientists, business executives, and the like, teaching its laypeople the sense in which every secular vocation—including, above all, the callings of husband, wife, and parent—is a sphere of Christian ministry, a way of serving God and neighbor that is grounded in God's truth." [8]

Gene Edward Veith

List projects or areas of service you did together with your child. What was the scope of your work? Where did you work? Record the date and as many details as possible:

_____

_____

_____

Describe a time your child worked hard to accomplish a huge task:

_____

_____

_____

Additional thoughts, observations, prayers, or memories:

_____

_____

_____

_____

_____

_____

_____

_____

_____

_____

DEVELOPED A
BIBLICAL VIEW OF MONEY

A significant portion of life revolves around money—working, saving, spending, planning, giving, and stressing over it. Financial wisdom is one of the most emphasized themes of the Bible and it should be in our home as well. The Bible has more than 2,000 verses about money, so God has alot to say about the topic. There is a direct correlation between how we handle money and our faith. We will either worship money or worship with our money. Jesus tells us, "For where your treasure is, there your heart will be also" (Luke 12:34). We try to teach our children that money is a good servant, but a poor master.

There are opportunities every day to financially disciple our children. A trip to the store will likely include the request from a child, "Can I buy it?" One of our children asks us "How much did you pay for it?" all the time. We have come to see these kinds of questions as opportunities to teach a biblical view of money. Here are five biblical principles children of all ages can learn:

God is the source and owner of all money. God gives us the ability to earn money, so everything we have ultimately is from Him (Deut. 8:18). Since God is the owner of all things, that means the money we earn belongs to God. He has asked us to faithfully manage His money, which the Bible calls stewardship. Many of Jesus' parables focus on being a good or poor steward and are good to read and discuss with your child.

◆ *Work diligently, manage wisely.* God commands us to work, which is a blessing to us and is for His glory, the good of others, and the provision of our family. Proverbs teaches that those who work hard to earn money, avoid debt, and save generally prosper financially. Those who are lazy and overextend themselves with debt often suffer poverty.

◆ *Fight for contentment.* Billions of marketing dollars are spent to convince your child not to be content. Many people think that having more money, an exotic vacation, or a fun toy would make them happy. Material things cannot satisfy our deepest longings—only God can. In our home, we have modeled this principle by being content to drive an older car, not chasing the latest technology, paying attention to the affections of our hearts, and removing items that capture our love over Christ. Contentment starts in the heart being thankful for what we have, not being focused on what we don't.

◆ *Make it your goal to be wise, not rich!* The Bible tells us that it is better to get wisdom than gold (Prov. 16:16) and that a good name is more desirable than great wealth (Prov. 22:1). "Do not weary yourself to gain wealth, cease from your consideration of it. When you set your eyes upon it, it is gone" (Prov. 23:4 NASB). We need to encourage our children to kill greed when it sprouts up (Col. 3:5).

◆ *Trust in God, not money.* A great threat posed by money is that those who have wealth are tempted to place their trust in it rather than in God. The Bible warns us that those who trust in riches will fall (Prov. 11:28).

Ways to teach children about money:

◆ *Use the jar or envelope method.* Provide children with a visual so they can see where money is going and how it is growing.

◆ *Provide opportunities to earn money.* Teach your child how to get a babysitting job, mow lawns, or do other small jobs so they have the opportunity to work for an employer.

◆ *Set a healthy example.* Money habits are developed when children are young, which is strongly impacted by our example as parents.

◆ *Give payments, not allowances.* When we grow up, we don't receive free money, so don't give your child a free allowance. Pay your children for chores or work around the home. Help your children learn that money is earned, and give them opportunities to work.

◆ *Avoid impulse buys.* If you take a child to the store, he or she will ask if they can buy something. Teach them to create a budget and plan a purchase. Encourage your child to wait on purchases and look for a deal.

◆ *Encourage giving.* Prioritize giving to your church. Also, consider picking a cause that excites your child and invite them to give. If they see someone in need and their heart is touched or they want to be exceedingly generous, do not discourage them.

◆ *Open a bank account.* When your child is a teenager, open a bank account to teach money management on a small and manageable scale.

◆ *Start a small business.* Children and teens have plenty of time, and what better way to use it than learning to make money. Our children have made a small business out of mowing and caring for pets, for example. Our ten-year-old learned to play taps on the bugle and has opportunities to play for military veterans, our eight-year-old learned to knit winter hats and sells them, and our fourteen-year-old learned to raise bees and chickens to sell honey and eggs.

Minding Your Own Business by Raymond and Dorothy Moore is filled with ideas and suggestions to help you in this area.

Share a memory of a time God provided for your family. What need was met? What were the circumstances?

_____

_____

_____

I modeled money management to my child in the following ways:

_____

_____

_____

Describe a time your child worked to earn money. What work did they do? How much money did they earn?

_____

_____

_____

Additional thoughts, observations, prayers, or memories:

_____

_____

_____

_____

_____

_____

KNOWS HOW TO CREATE
A BUDGET AND MANAGE MONEY

My (Josh) first entrepreneurial experience occurred as an eight-year-old when my brother Jake and I made paper watches and went door to door selling our creations. They looked like what you would expect from an eight-year-old—crooked lines, imperfect coloring, and of course, they did not keep time. The watches were worthless, but our kind neighbors purchased them anyway, and we went home with a small stack of cash and a valuable lesson learned. My parents had taught us to create a basic budget using the 80/10/10 rule, which is a good guide to teach children. We took our watch money and placed 10 percent in the giving envelope, 10 percent in the savings envelope, and 80 percent in the spend envelope. The principles I learned as a child created habits that have aided me as an adult. Jen and I made our first home purchase using the envelope method. When it was time to pay the down payment, we literally handed them a stack of cash from an envelope. The envelope method helped us budget, track spending, and develop self-control.

A budget is simply a spending plan, a way to track all expenses, and manage money. The Bible tells us that "The plans of the diligent lead surely to abundance" (Prov. 21:5). The unwise person runs out of money because he spends quickly and carelessly. "Everyone who is hasty comes surely to poverty" (Prov. 21:5). Now is the time for a child to learn how to make a plan for their money, no matter how small the amount. Teach your child to make a simple budget using three categories: Give generously, save aggressively, and spend wisely. If you are looking for a helpful resource consider *Your Kids Can Master Their Money* by Ron and Judy Blue and Jeremy White or *Smart Money Smart Kids* by Dave Ramsey and Rachel Cruze.

Give generously: Children should learn that everything belongs to the Lord, so we give our first and best to Him. In the early days, include your children when you give by allowing them to put money into the offering plate at church and to participate in helping others in need. Our family worked together to raise money for another family who needed a new vehicle and it helped our children learn the joy of giving to others. As children get older, encourage them to give to church and to any charity they are passionate about.

Save aggressively: All children need to learn how to save and invest money. Train children to save for items so they learn the habit needed to save for a car, home, education, and retirement. For beginners, use the envelope method so they can physically place money in its proper envelope; as they get older open a bank account. Teach your child how the stock market works, how to invest money, and the power of compound interest. Help your young adult begin to invest money as early as possible.

Spend wisely: Some children have the tendency to want to spend every penny as soon as they get it. Teach children to delay gratification, to shop with a list, and not to make impulsive or extravagant purchases but spend what his or her budget allows. Track spending for a month so that a young person can see how money is being spent. Older children can be introduced to a more detailed budget by creating spending categories such as transportation, clothes, food, entertainment, and education. A simple online search will provide you with a customizable template for creating a budget.

What systems did you use to help your child begin a pattern of giving, saving, and spending?

_____

_____

_____

Write a summary of your child's first written budget. Include the date, their age, amount of income, expenses, and the amount of money they aim to give, save and spend:

_____

_____

_____

Describe a time your child saved their money over a length of time for a planned purchase. What was your child saving for? How much did the item cost? How long did it take him or her to reach the goal?

_____

_____

_____

Ask your child what places or organizations they would like to give money to and why. Record his or her answers here:

_____

_____

_____

Additional thoughts, observations, prayers, or memories:

_____

_____

UNDERSTANDS THE DANGER OF DEBT

Financial warning is a theme emphasized in Scripture that our children need to understand. The Bible has numerous cautions about the danger of debt, telling us it becomes a merciless master that leads to bondage. The Bible warns against the pitfalls of debt: "The borrower is the slave of the lender" (Prov. 22:7). Unfortunately, debt has become a normal way of life for many people. The average person aged eighteen to twenty-three has thousands of dollars of credit card and car debt, which increases with their age. Many individuals experience problems in life because of poor financial decisions, which can be long lasting.

Many financial problems are rooted in spiritual problems such as greed, laziness, or seeking happiness from the wrong source. We think we want a new television, a new car, or a fun adventure. What we really want is the person we were created for—Jesus. Nothing less will satisfy. Train your child to delay gratification, to save for purchases, and to be content with little. Here are some principles to teach related to debt.

◈ *Learn the secret of contentment.* We can be thankful for whatever material possessions God gives us, knowing that true riches are found in redemption in

Christ. Contentment works not by adding to our possessions, but by subtracting from our desires.

💎 *Avoid debt by saving and anticipating future expenses.* Those who lack wisdom spend all their money and have nothing left for emergencies, creating a crisis when an unplanned problem inevitably arises. Saving provides protection from future calamities such as unemployment, disability, or an unexpected repair to a home or car. One contemporary means of preparing for future problems is to acquire health, life, auto, and home insurance. Explore these subjects with your child so he or she understands each of them.

💎 *Understand credit cards.* When a child turns eighteen, he or she will begin getting credit card offers. If your child has not learned to avoid debt, they will become another credit card victim.

💎 *Gambling is unwise and harmful.* Gambling undermines God's methods by encouraging people to earn money without working for it. Gambling is poor stewardship of God's resources. Only two things can happen with gambling: money is foolishly wasted or money is won by defrauding other people. The Bible tells us "Wealth gained hastily will dwindle, but whoever gathers little by little will increase it" (Prov. 13:11).

💎 *Live within your means.* Wise people don't spend money they don't have. "He who loves pleasure will be a poor man" (Prov. 21:17). Establish a means of earning before taking on financial responsibility.

Tell about a time your child wanted to purchase something but didn't have the money. What valuable lessons were learned?

_____

_____

_____

Has somebody in your family suffered because of bankruptcy, credit card debt, or gambling addiction? How has that affected your family or child?

_____

_____

_____

Additional thoughts, observations, prayers, or memories:

_____

_____

_____

_____

_____

_____

_____

_____

_____

_____

KNOWS HOW TO
MANAGE TIME WISELY

"If you read history, you will find that the Christians who did the most for the present world were just those who thought most of the next. The apostles themselves, who set on foot the conversion of the Roman Empire, the great men who built up the Middle Ages, the English evangelicals who abolished the slave trade, all left their mark on earth, precisely because their minds were occupied with heaven. It is since Christians have largely ceased to think of the other world that they have become so ineffective in this," states C.S. Lewis.[9]

The Bible reminds us that life is short, like a vapor or blade of grass, so that we will order our time for what matters most in eternity (Jas. 4:14; Ps. 39:4–5). Scripture reminds us to count our days so that we do not waste the time we have been given by God (Ps. 90:12). We are to use our time wisely, from our early days to our last breath. There is no such thing as retirement in God's economy. To be alive is to be fruitful for the Lord (Ps. 92:12–14). Children need to be taught to reject the idea that life is about leisure and self-indulgence, and learn to wisely steward their time to serve the Lord. The death and resurrection of Jesus changes how we view and use time: "He died for all, that those who live might no longer live for themselves but for Him who for their sake died and was raised" (2 Cor. 5:15).

We can train our children to ask themselves when they come to the end of their life, "What kind of life lived would cause Jesus to say to us, "Well done, good and faithful servant?"

God created time as a tool to be stewarded. Like any resource, we can use time well or we can waste it. God dislikes laziness and wants us to be industrious in that we see what needs to be done and work to accomplish it. Good time management begins with a biblical view of time and the conviction to live accordingly. Children can be taught good time management by learning the following principles:

- Clearly define priorities. Schedule what matters most first or it will be pushed out by less important, urgent matters that arise daily. Opportunities related to spiritual priorities always take precedence! We have done this with our children by purchasing them a fun paper planner around the age of ten. We have also taught them to use a watch with a calendar feature.

- Jesus shows us how to order our time. He didn't say yes to every need, but focused on doing the work God gave Him to do (John 17:4). Paul instructs us, "Look carefully how you walk . . . making the best use of the time" (Eph. 5:15–16). Help children learn to say no to good things so they can say yes to the best things.

- Help your child develop an eternal perspective of time. Thinking about eternity helps to eliminate the vanities from life and to focus our time on what matters most.

- The discipline of planning is highly recommended in the Bible (Luke 14:28). Proverbs 14:22 (NIV) says, "Those who plan what is good find love and faithfulness." Train children to set goals, write them down, and celebrate when they are accomplished.

- God gave six days for working and one day for resting. We can train our children to order their time each week according to God's design.

Time management skills are learned in practical ways such as when a child wakes up on time by themselves, is able to get dressed and leave by a set time, and has the freedom to meet homework deadlines. A watch and alarm clocks are great gift ideas that teach children time management. Allow children to experience the consequences of poor time management.

What tools have you given your child, such as a watch or calendar, to help them learn to manage time wisely? When did you give them and for what purpose?

_____

_____

_____

Does your family observe a sabbath or day of rest on Sundays? If so, describe how your family uses that time. If not, what does your family do to unwind and relax?

_____

_____

_____

Additional thoughts, observations, prayers, or memories:

_____

_____

_____

_____

_____

_____

_____

_____

CHAPTER 14

HOME MANAGEMENT

KNOWS HOW TO
COOK SIMPLE MEALS

O ne thing every person in the world has in common is that we all eat breakfast, lunch, dinner, snacks, and desserts! The ability to prepare and cook food for oneself and for others is an essential skill that not only will be needed to become an independent adult but can be used to be a blessing to one's family and friends. We encourage our children to make wise decisions with food and to learn how to prepare food for themselves and their siblings from a young age. While keeping children safe in the kitchen is essential, you can encourage them to enjoy using kitchen tools and appliances when age appropriate.

I (Jen) will never forget the time Josh and I came home from a neighborhood meeting to a messy kitchen and a pile of warm chocolate-chip cookies on the counter. Our ten-year-old son, Asher, had decided to surprise us with his homemade creations while we were out! He was developing his kitchen skills and was incredibly proud of the cookies, even serving them to us on fancy china dishes. One taste of the cookies, though, proved something had gone awry with the recipe! The cookies looked and smelled beautiful, but tasted awful! After looking through the recipe together, our son discovered that he added one *cup* of baking soda to the recipe instead of one *teaspoon*! We all enjoyed a good laugh about the cookies, but valuable learning occurred that day. Asher celebrated the success of independently using the mixer, oven, and baking his cookies, but learned the importance of reading recipes in detail and recognizing that each ingredient—and the amount—matters.

Consider the following when teaching your child to prepare and cook simple recipes:

◈ *Begin teaching your child food preparation when they are as young as toddlers.* Keep healthy snacks and unbreakable dishes within their reach. In our home we keep a cupboard of healthy snacks, plastic bowls, and cups in a low drawer. The bottom drawer of our refrigerator is designated for easy-to-grab snack foods such as apples, string cheese, and yogurt.

◈ *Introduce meal preparation with simple ingredients and tools.* Experiment with making peanut butter and jelly sandwiches, peanut butter on celery, designing a charcuterie board of precut meats and cheeses, preparing no-bake cookies, combining ingredients for trail mix and yogurt parfaits. These are all examples of foods that require preparation but little cutting or cooking. Mastery of food preparation and cleanup will make future cooking much easier and will build confidence.

◈ *Cook together before cooking independently.* Before allowing your child to cook independently, invite your child to cook with you. I have yet to meet a child who will refuse the invitation to help bake chocolate-chip cookies or stir pancake batter! Give your child the freedom to actively take part in the cooking process by getting out pots and pans, measuring and pouring ingredients, turning on the oven or stove top, cracking eggs, chopping vegetables, operating small appliances such as a stand mixer or griddle, watching for water to boil, setting the cooking timer, or stirring sauces. Gradually increase their level of skill to using sharp knives, taking things in or out of the oven, and flipping pancakes.

◆ *Provide simple recipes and let them go!* Pancakes, boxed macaroni and cheese, quick breads, cookies, smoothies, jello, and eggs are all simple foods your child can cook with basic skills. Stay near them while cooking, but resist the urge to hover. Offer help when needed, celebrate success, laugh together at the funny things that happen, and trouble-shoot failures.

◆ *Invite your child to plan and prepare a weekly family meal.* Cooking for others gives greater meaning and enjoyment to the task of preparing food. Help your child plan, shop for, and prepare a family meal. Depending on your child's age and interest level, consider making this a weekly or monthly tradition.

◆ *Teach your child to cook heirloom family recipes.* Our family has a handful of favorite recipes that are enjoyed regularly and at holidays. Help your child master these recipes so they will be able to enjoy them and teach them to their own children in the future.

What were the first foods and recipes you taught your child to prepare? How old was your child? Did you enjoy eating the food together also? Include as many details as possible:

_____

_____

_____

What was the first recipe your child cooked all by themselves? How did it taste? Did your child enjoy the experience?

_____

_____

_____

_____

_____

Include a photo of your child with their finished dish:

Does your family have heirloom recipes that have been handed down from generation to generation? Share those here. Include a recipe card with instructions if possible:

_____

_____

Additional thoughts, observations, prayers, or memories:

The ability to prepare and cook food for
oneself and for others is an essential skill
 that not only will be needed to become
an independent adult but can be used to
be a blessing to one's family and friends.

KNOWS HOW TO CLEAN THE HOUSE AND DO LAUNDRY

When I (Jen) went off to college I lived in a dorm where four ladies shared one private bathroom and a mini-kitchen. We were assigned cleaning chores and required to pass an inspection for our assignment each week. I had never been tasked with formal cleaning in a household setting until these inspections. I remember my roommate showing me how to clean the bathroom, and I was unsure how to clean our room's large metal mini-blinds when given this assignment at the end of the year. Each weekend I would take my laundry home for my mother to clean, and it wasn't until I was married and lived in my first apartment that I did laundry on my own. I clearly was not properly equipped with cleaning and laundry skills! Fast-forward to today, I have honed my skills and our household is in order. Our children flourish with taking ownership of cleaning and laundry tasks, and the same can be true for yours.

Cleaning

Teaching children to clean and do other household chores should be simple and no-nonsense. Elaborate, color-coded, revolving chores charts are unnecessary, complicated and require more maintenance than they are worth. Instead, opt for assigning children one or two simple daily tasks and change their job as abilities expand. If you have multiple children and give each child one or two daily cleaning tasks, each child will learn how to master a multitude of skills during their years at home, and your house will remain adequately tidy.

The following are examples of daily tasks by age.

Toddler/preschool: Make bed, pick up and put away toys, tidy shoes by the entry door, feed the dog or cat, and wipe door handles or walls with a washcloth.

Elementary: Unload and reload the dishwasher, take out garbage, vacuum, wipe appliances and kitchen cabinets, dusting.

Middle and high school: Sweep and mop floors, shovel snow, mow grass, and clean bathrooms.

To give you a glimpse of how this plays out practically, our five children each have one daily job they are required to complete before and after school each day. In the mornings our high school student feeds the chickens and collects eggs; our junior higher takes out the garbage; our fourth-grader unloads and reloads the dishwasher; our second-grader feeds the outdoor cats and tidies the back entryway; our kindergartener picks up stray items left in the living room. The afternoon routine is similar with one job per person. Completing the same task every day is simple. It becomes a matter of routine, and each child is able to master their skill and take ownership over its completion.

Other tips to teach cleaning:

◆ *One day per week, take a couple of hours of "all hands on deck" cleaning time.* Deep clean bathrooms, floors, and walls, and dust surfaces. Our children are each assigned a room or task each week. During this time I am hands-on with teaching and supervising.

◆ *Assemble the best cleaning tools.* Cleaning floors will be frustrating if you don't have an adequate broom, vacuum, and mop. Purchase enough cleaning supplies for everyone to clean at the same time. This includes a healthy supply of scrub brushes, wash cloths, paper towels, and cleaning products.

◆ *Set realistic expectations.* If a cleaning job is difficult for you, it will be more difficult for your child. Show them how to clean tricky messes like dog hair on a rug or food burned on a stove top. Don't expect professional results, and celebrate all work done with a joyful spirit!

Laundry

Similar to cleaning, laundry is best done when the routine is simple. Utilize the following tips to teach your child how to care for their clothing and eventually wash, dry, and put away all of their own laundry.

◆ *Give every member of the family their own laundry basket,* even if children share the same bedroom. Wash and dry each load of laundry according to whom it belongs to. This eliminates the need to constantly be sorting and making separate piles of clean clothes. Show little ones how to put their dirty clothes into their own basket and how to put their clean socks and pants into drawers. Once those skills are mastered, graduate to hanging up shirts and dresses. Allow elementary-age children and teenagers to hang up and put away their entire basket of clean clothes.

◆ *Teach your child how to use the washer and dryer.* Explain the various machine settings for washing and drying as well as symbols on clothing labels. If it is helpful, consider hanging a chart of laundry symbols and their meaning. Demonstrate how full to fill the washing machine. Keep detergent accessible. If you are concerned about your child spilling or using too much laundry soap or softener, utilize detergent pods or wool dryer balls.

◆ *Set expectations and give your child the freedom to wash their own laundry.* Choose a desired age when you feel your child is responsible to care for their own laundry. Communicate expectations around how often you'd like your child to wash, dry, and put away their clothes. Help with this transition by giving loving reminders, transferring their clothes to the dryer if needed, and offering plenty of encouragement for a job well done!

Describe the daily or weekly cleaning tasks you assigned to your child at the following ages.

Age 3–5:

_____

_____

Age 6–10:

_____

_____

Age 11–14:

_____

_____

Age 15–18:

_____

_____

Record the date your child learned how to
Unload and reload the dishwasher:

_____

Put away laundry:

_____

Use the vacuum cleaner:

_____

Take out garbage:

_____

Clean a toilet:

_____

Mop the floor:

_____

Clean the oven:

_____

_____

_____

Wash and dry their laundry:

_____

_____

_____

Additional thoughts, observations, prayers, or memories:

_____

_____

_____

_____

KNOWS HOW TO USE COMMON TOOLS AND HAS BASIC SEWING SKILLS

astering the art of using basic household tools will serve your child well throughout their life. We have all been in the situation where a button pops off a shirt or a household repair is needed. Having the skills to confidently tackle these small tasks avoids catastrophe and stress, and saves both the time and money of seeking professional help. When teaching your child how to use tools, be sure to teach these skills to both your sons and daughters. Future adult women need to know how to wield a drill and hammer. Likewise, adult men should know how to use an iron and do basic mending.

Our top ten essential household tools and sewing skills to learn:

1. Hammer and nails
2. Screw driver
3. Electric drill
4. Tape measure
5. Paint brush and roller

6. Ladder skills
7. Power tools such as circular saw, nail or staple gun, electric sander
8. Sewing a button
9. Ironing fabric
10. Basic machine sewing

Invite your child to help when you are using tools or doing a sewing project. When children are little, helping can be handing you tools or supplies while you work, helping you choose materials, or finalizing project design elements. As children get older, invite them to use tools in small ways, under your direct supervision.

Teach safety and caution. Remind your child of the dangers of hammering their thumb or sewing their fingers. Always have your child wear protective eyewear and gloves when appropriate. I (Josh) worked in custom cabinetry for two years, and many of my colleagues were missing a finger because they cut it off with a power tool. Power tools are a blessing, but it only takes one careless second for a serious injury, so teach older children to go slow, be cautious, and always think safety.

Give your child tools as gifts. Consider adding tools, a toolbox, a sewing machine, scissors, and thread to your child's birthday and Christmas gifts. Include age-appropriate books about building, sewing, and creating to inspire your child's creativity.

Enjoy the art of practicing. The following combinations of tools and supplies will give your child endless hours of fun and build independence in learning how to use tools. Keep raw materials around your home for a child to utilize.

- Box of nails + hammer + thick board
- Box of screws + drill + thick board
- Paint + roller + drywall
- Tape measure + pencil + handsaw

- Needle + thread + buttons
- Fabric + cutting mat + straight edge + rotary cutter
- Wrinkled fabric + iron

◆ *Give your child the freedom to build and create using tools.* At the age of nine, our daughter learned needle skills by making cross-stitch art. She also used the sewing machine to make hair scrunchies for her friends. At the age of ten, our boys loved assembling furniture from big-box stores such as IKEA. They built their own shelving and dressers for their bedroom. At the age of fourteen, our sons were partners in painting interior and exterior walls, hanging art, building beehives, skillfully using a paint brush, ladder, hammer, nails, and drill.

◆ *If you are not confident in your own skills with household tools or at sewing, learn how to do these things together.* Take a class or spend time learning from skilled grandparents. Our girls learned the art of quilt binding from their Grammie. Making memories and learning together was a delight to everyone.

◆ *Hone your new skills by creating gifts for others.* Use a hammer and nails to create string art. Cut logs to make Christmas ornaments. Sew fabric into coasters. Quilt a small table runner or place mat.

What tools or sewing materials did your purchase with the intent of teaching your child to use them:

_____

_____

Describe the skills your child learned using household tools or sewing. Did your child make something to use or give as a gift? Record the date of what they learned and what they made:

_____

_____

_____

_____

_____

Which skills did your child most enjoy learning? How can you encourage your child to develop those skills further?

_____

_____

Take a photo of something your child made and place it below.

Additional thoughts, observations, prayers, or memories:

_____

_____

_____

CONFIDENT AS A HOST OR GUEST

Hospitality is more than meals; it is freely inviting people into our lives and homes, serving others joyfully with ease, welcoming strangers, providing warmth, giving a place of rest, and showing our love for others with good food and conversation. Showing hospitality is a first step in sharing Christ's love and the Gospel with others. Practicing hospitality is sharing your life with others on a deeper level than would be experienced in a public gathering. Inviting others into your home is showing your guests how you live and what you value.

Ideas for teaching hospitality:

- Make a list of people you and your child would like to invite to your home. The invitation can be for a play date, meal, outdoor activity, or any activity you choose.

- Offer to host a special celebration for a loved one, such as a birthday party or bridal or baby shower. Allow your child to plan facets of the party such as games or food.

- Strategically invite friends out to a restaurant for an impromptu meal or dessert after church or a sports game.

◈ Invite friends or family over for a casual evening of board games, a movie, or a bonfire.

◈ Before hosting guests, take an honest look around your home or child's bedroom together. Discuss whether the decor, artwork, and items in view reflect your love of Christ—or do they tell another story?

When preparing to host, do the following things together:

◈ Give forethought to the menu or supplies you will need.

◈ Ask your guests about food preferences or allergies.

◈ Make your guests comfortable. Clear a place for everyone to sit. Clean the bathrooms and floors. Move pets to another room. Emphasize that perfection isn't the goal.

◈ Prepare for your guests before they arrive. Don't be hunting for spare dishes and getting folding chairs from the basement after their arrival.

◈ Greet your guests at the door. Welcome them, offer to hang up their coat, and communicate your pleasure at having them in your home.

◈ Serve with a smile. Practice phrases such as "What can I get you?" "Oh no, don't get up!" and "Who needs seconds?"

◈ Share family favorites. Prepare a family recipe and invite your guests to experience whatever traditions are special to you.

Learning to be an excellent guest is just as important as being a good host. A good guest will make their host feel valued and appreciated. Remind your child of the following suggestions when visiting family and friends:

◆ Arrive on time.

◆ Offer to bring something such as a side dish or appetizer.

◆ Be complimentary of the host's food and home.

◆ Say please and thank you.

◆ Offer to help with clean-up or preparing food.

◆ Acknowledge your host's gift of hospitality by saying thank you afterward.

The Bible gives countless examples of hospitality. Read the following passages together. Note your observations about what it looks like to show hospitality from a biblical perspective.

Genesis 18:1–8, Abraham and the three visitors:

_____

_____

_____

1 Kings 17:7–16, Elijah receives the hospitality of the widow of Zarephath:

_____

_____

_____

Luke 10:38–41, Mary and Martha:

_____

_____

_____

Luke 19:1–6, Zaccheus:

_____

_____

_____

Acts 16:11–15, Lydia:

_____

_____

_____

Matthew 25:42–43, Jesus:

_____

_____

_____

Hebrews 13:1–2, the early church:

_____

_____

_____

Make a list together of the people your child would like to invite
to your home:

_____

_____

_____

Share a memory of a dinner, party, or event you planned to show hospitality.
What was the event? Who was invited? What food did you serve?

_____

_____

_____

Walk through your home and your child's bedroom together. Discuss with your child whether the items in your home reflect your love of Jesus Christ. What should be removed? What could be added?

_____

_____

_____

Take a photo of your child's bedroom and keep a copy here:

Additional thoughts, observations, prayers, or memories:

_____

_____

_____

_____

_____

KNOWS HOW TO CARE FOR THE LAWN, GARDEN, AND OUTDOORS

When I (Jen) was a girl, both my mother and grandpa loved being outdoors caring for their gardens, lawn, and landscaping. I can recall countless hours spent with my grandpa in his garden, and with my mom meticulously choosing and caring for her perennial gardens. The smell of dirt, fertilizer, fresh flowers, and vegetables are still crisp in my mind. I enjoyed our outdoor time together, and these moments inspired me, as an adult, to spend a summer working in a professional greenhouse and to continually experiment with gardening and growing plants at our home. When I am outdoors, tending to God's creation around me, I am reminded of the Garden of Eden. In Genesis, God uses a garden as the setting by which he gave a beautiful picture of His complete love, perfect creation, and provision for us. He charged Adam and Eve to tend the garden, and have dominion over the earth, in Genesis 2:15. Knowing how to care for the outdoors and keep a garden has helped to provide food for our family, transform landscaping in our fixer-upper house, and bring joy to friends and neighbors with cut flowers and the gifts of our garden's bounty.

No matter where you live, there is always an opportunity to teach your child how to keep plants, grow a small garden, and to help maintain outdoor spaces. Learning to oversee and maintain nature around us teaches practical life skills and will point your child toward Christ as he or she experiences the work of tending to their own lawns and gardens.

The little years:

- 💎 *Help water* indoor or outdoor plants.

- 💎 *Observe the seasons together.* Bring your child outside with you as you tend to seasonal tasks such as raking leaves, shoveling the sidewalks, or filling bird feeders.

- 💎 *Pull weeds, pick up rocks or sticks.* Little hands are excellent at pulling weeds in the garden or picking up rocks and sticks in the springtime.

- 💎 *Bring your child to a garden center* and allow them to look around and enjoy, and choose a plant. Plant it together and watch it grow.

Elementary years:

- 💎 *Introduce your child to simple lawn and garden tools* such as rakes, shovels, hoes, and wheelbarrows. Work alongside one another using these tools so your child will gain familiarity and precision.

- 💎 *Plan and grow a garden together.* Grow veggies and flowers in pots on your balcony or windowsill, if you are tight on space. Alternatively, plant a full pizza garden or pumpkin patch if you have room to spare. Utilize books filled with creative gardening ideas that will both teach and inspire creativity such as *Roots, Shoots, Buckets & Boots* by Sharon Lovejoy or *Easy Peasy: Gardening for Kids* by Kirsten Bradley.

- 💎 *Keep a sketchbook or journal together* of your gardening and growing endeavors.

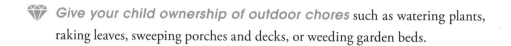 *Give your child ownership of outdoor chores* such as watering plants, raking leaves, sweeping porches and decks, or weeding garden beds.

Middle and high school years:

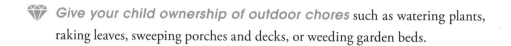 *Teach your child how to use outdoor power tools* such as lawnmowers, weed eaters, leaf blowers, garden tillers, and snow blowers. Allow your child to observe you operate the tool, then give the child the opportunity to use it with direct supervision until they have fully mastered the tool. Teach your child to wear protective eyewear, to keep their fingers away from all moving elements, and to move slowly.

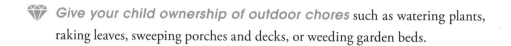 *Give your child the responsibility of weekly outdoor chores* such as mowing the lawn or shoveling sidewalks.

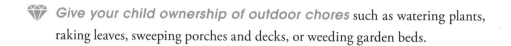 *Work together on large-scale lawn and garden projects* such as dividing or planting trees and shrubs, building landscaping borders, or cleaning gutters.

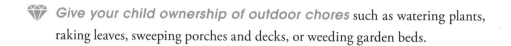 *Encourage your child to offer their outdoor skills for hire*. Mowing lawns, shoveling driveways and sidewalks, or landscaping are all excellent ways for your child to earn money and hone their skills.

Make a list of the flowers and plants you would like to grow together. Where will you plant them? What supplies do you need? After you have grown them, describe the process. How did your plants grow? What would you do differently next time?

_____

_____

_____

_____

_____

Record the date and special memories of your child learning to use the following lawn and garden tools.

Rake:

_____

_____

Shovel:

_____

_____

Hoe:

_____

_____

Weed eater:

_____

_____

Leaf blower:

_____

_____

Lawn mower:

_____

_____

Snow blower:

_____

_____

_____

Take a photo of your child working in the yard, garden, or outdoors. Keep a copy here:

Additional thoughts, observations, prayers, or memories:

_____

_____

_____

_____

_____

_____

_____

_____

_____

_____

_____

The Lord God took the man
and put him in the garden of Eden
to work it and keep it.

Genesis 2:15

CHAPTER 15

PERSONAL CARE

TAUGHT MANNERS
AND KNOWS COMMON ETIQUETTE

Emily Post, the queen of etiquette, states "Nobody wakes up in the morning and says, 'I think I'll be rude today.' Most of us think of ourselves as polite, but when we're in a hurry or dealing with strangers we don't always use the manners we know we should."[10] I think it's safe to say that we all have been in situations where we weren't prepared to navigate the appropriate etiquette required for the event we were attending. Attending a formal dinner, wedding, or funeral, or participating in cultural traditions requires its own set of norms for what is and is not appropriate. It is impossible to prepare your child for each and every occasion, but having a basic knowledge of common etiquette will help steer your child in the right direction. Ideally, excellent manners will become a habit for your child. The following is a list of ten essential etiquette skills we have chosen to teach our children:

1. Saying please and thank you.

2. Holding doors for others.

3. Address adults as Mr. or Mrs. when appropriate.

4. Saying "Excuse me," instead of interrupting.

5. Sneezing or coughing into an arm rather than a hand.

6. Graciously saying "No, thank you."

7. Smiling, displaying a pleasant demeanor, and looking others in the eye when speaking.

8. Answering questions with a question. For example, if an adult asks, "How are you?" the child would respond with, "I'm excellent! How are you?"

9. Making introductions.

10. Table etiquette: Napkin in lap, use of glasses and flatware, reaching, and chewing with one's mouth closed.

The hands-on, how-to of teaching manners involves consistent gentle reminders and opportunities to put skills into practice. Consider doing the following activities together to build fluency and confidence in the area of etiquette.

◆ **Read books together about etiquette.** Read small sections aloud when teaching specific skills or use as a reference manual as needed. Good basic books include *Manners Begin at Breakfast* by Princess Marie-Chantal of Greece, *Etiquette* by Emily Post, *Emily Post's Etiquette: Manners for Today* by Lizzie Post and Daniel Post Senning.

◆ **Take an etiquette class.** Community education programs in many cities offer basic etiquette classes. Sometimes classes include activities such as a formal dinner or tea party.

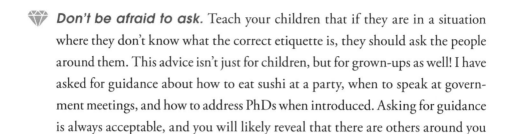

Don't be afraid to ask. Teach your children that if they are in a situation where they don't know what the correct etiquette is, they should ask the people around them. This advice isn't just for children, but for grown-ups as well! I have asked for guidance about how to eat sushi at a party, when to speak at government meetings, and how to address PhDs when introduced. Asking for guidance is always acceptable, and you will likely reveal that there are others around you with the same question.

Always say thank you. Teaching your child to say thank you is teaching your child to communicate that they value the actions, gifts, conversation, skills, and presence of the people they interact with. A thank-you can be saying thank you in person, with a phone call, in text message or in handwritten note. If given a gift, say thank you accordingly. The following are our personal thank-you guidelines:

- The hospitality of a friend should be given a verbal thank you along with a text message.
- A birthday or Christmas gift sent in the mail from a friend or relative should invoke an immediate phone call.
- A gift opened at a birthday party or an act or service should receive both a verbal and written thank you note.

Make a list of etiquette skills you would like your child to have.

_____

_____

_____

Describe the fun and creative ways you taught manners. Record special memories you made together while learning:

_____

_____

_____

Describe a time you observed your child displaying excellent manners. How old were they? What was the circumstance? Include as many details as possible:

_____

_____

_____

Additional thoughts, observations, prayers, or memories:

_____

_____

_____

_____

_____

_____

_____

_____

_____

_____

TAUGHT PERSONAL HYGIENE AND MAINTAINS A GOOD APPEARANCE

Teaching your children to care for their body by learning and practicing good personal hygiene encourages your child be an excellent steward of what God has given them. 1 Corinthians 6:19–20 says, "Do you not know that your body is a temple of the Holy Spirit within you, whom you have from God? You are not your own; for you were bought with a price. So glorify God in your body." This principle can be easily illustrated for your child at any age. Ask your child to name an item they love. Now ask your child how they would feel if that item was left outside in the rain and mud, only to become dirty, smelly, and broken. My guess is that your child would be heartbroken. The same attention and care should be given to our bodies. Our bodies are temples of the Holy Spirit, bought at a price through the death of Jesus Christ, and are to be used to give honor to God. Because we matter to God, caring for His creation, our bodies, should be taken seriously. The way an individual cares for his or her body not only reflects Christ, but can also affect your children's self-image, how others view them, and their health.

The little years:

◆ *Start with the basics: teach excellent handwashing.* My mother used to say, "Dirty hands spread gross things! Wash them!" Introduce your child to the concept of germs. Task your child with washing his or her hands regularly such as before cooking and eating, and after using the restroom, touching animals, and coughing or sneezing. Experiment with teaching handwashing in fun ways such as singing songs to measure how long a child washes, providing fun soaps, or intentionally making messes with your hands and then washing them off.

◈ *Establish routines and expectations.* Children form habits for personal cleanliness when they are young. Establish simple bedtime, bath-time, and morning routines to begin the habits of teeth brushing, bathing, combing hair, and wearing clean clothing.

◈ *As your child is able, invite him or her to help with hygiene tasks.* These can include putting his or her own toothpaste on a toothbrush, getting out a comb, putting away a brush, and choosing their clothing or pajamas. Be alert for tasks your child is able to do and invite them to attempt new skills.

◈ *Give your child tools for success.* Keep a stool in the bathroom so your child will easily be able to wash his or her hands before eating and after using the restroom. Store toothbrushes in a low drawer. Arrange your child's clothing in a way that they are able to choose their own socks and pajamas.

◈ *Enjoy this time together.* Make learning fun and memorable. Have your child take bubble baths with big bubbles, purchase fun barrettes and bows for styling girls' hair, select toothpaste that tastes delicious, and play in mud puddles just for the opportunity to clean up afterward!

The elementary years:

◈ *Teach your child how to take a shower.* Gradually give greater independence with bathing. Show your child the difference between shampoo, conditioner, and body wash.

◈ *Help children learn to style their hair.* Girls should learn to comb and style their hair when it is both wet and dry. A Wet Brush is a lifesaver for girls who are learning to brush long, wet hair. Teach them to use barrettes, ponytail holders and clips, and to make braids. If you have long hair, encourage your daughters to practice their skills on you. Boys should know how to use a comb and brush as appropriate.

◈ *Continue to monitor teeth brushing.* Model proper brushing technique, toothpaste amounts, rinsing, and flossing. We have found that electronic toothbrushes are a worthwhile investment for children as they monitor the amount of time a child spends brushing and the vibrations provide a thorough cleaning experience.

◈ *Talk about good smells and bad smells.* We've all met somebody who looks good but smells bad. Unchanged underwear, bad breath, and dirty clothing can all produce unpleasant body smells. Help your child gain greater awareness in this area. Keep these conversations lighthearted and avoid making statements that would cause your child to feel unnecessarily self-conscious.

◈ *Give your child the responsibility of making their own daily clothing choices.* This includes putting on clean clothing and undergarments. Help your child determine whether clothes are clean or dirty. Monitor whether your child is wearing clean clothing and ask each morning if they are wearing clean underwear.

Junior high and high school:

◈ *Continue to give insight, but do not control.* During these years, your child will move toward independence in the area of personal hygiene. Your child's personal style will develop, influencing their fashion and hairstyle choices, but your input is still greatly needed. Even if your child does not ask for your suggestions, continue to lovingly guide their choices in a way that advice is not interpreted as criticism.

◈ *Supply your child with the personal care products they need.* Keep a healthy supply of deodorant, facial cleanser, feminine products, or anything else your child regularly needs on hand. This will alleviate emergency trips to the store and will give your child permission to freely utilize the products they need.

◈ *Teach your child gender-specific hygiene practices.* Young men should know how to shave their face and properly apply cologne. Young ladies should learn how to properly use makeup, heated hairstyling tools, razors, and feminine products such as sanitary napkins, tampons, and pantyliners.

Describe your child's hairstyle, favorite pieces of clothing, and physical appearance.

The little years:

_____

_____

The elementary years:

_____

_____

Junior high and high school years:

_____

_____

Does your child love extra bubbles and extended bath time? Do you sing a song to remember how long to brush their teeth? Does your toddler climb up on a stool to wash his or her hands, yet still barely reach the faucet? Record precious memories of your little one here:

_____

_____

_____

Additional thoughts, observations, prayers, or memories:

_____

_____

_____

_____

_____

_____

_____

_____

_____

_____

KNOWS HOW TO
RESPOND IN AN EMERGENCY

N
o one likes to think about life-altering emergencies. But out of wisdom, we should prepare our children for them. Every family needs to talk about what to do in an emergency and where important information can be found. Take a moment and imagine an emergency such as an injury, abduction, or disaster; would your children, young or old, know what to do if they found themselves in this scenario? We never know when an emergency will occur or what it will be. Our children need some basic knowledge so they can keep their cool, think calmly, and solve problems quickly.

When I (Josh) was eleven years old, I found myself in an emergency. A group of friends gathered on a brisk fall day in my treehouse along the creek in my backyard. We lit a candle to warm our hands, but when I handed it to a friend, hot wax dripped on him and he instinctively dropped it. The candle landed on the second floor of the treehouse, rolled to an opening, and fell to the first floor. I remember thinking that there was no way the candle would still be lit after all that, but to my horror, it was not only still burning but had quickly ignited the prairie grass we used for a floor. Before I knew it, the flames had engulfed the first floor and were making their way up to the second floor, where I was sitting. My friends jumped and ran away leaving me all alone. The first thought that went through my head was to put out the fire so my parents wouldn't know what had happened.

I jumped from the second story, hit the ground with a thud, and began trying to stomp out the fire, which was now as wide as a bedroom and growing. The fire was so hot that it burnt off my eyebrows, eyelashes, and the front half of my hair. When I realized that I couldn't put out the fire, I sprinted to the house to get help. My dad calmly grabbed every hose we owned, put them together, and stretched them the half acre to the fire and put it out. Neighbors gathered to watch, someone called the fire department, which arrived after the fire was smoldering, and had a stern talk with me about the danger of fire.

My parents taught me to "get help" as soon as possible, and that advice may have saved a house from burning down that day. There are some emergencies that are self-generated, like mine, and others that are not of our doing. Children need to be prepared for both.

- *Discuss a family emergency plan.* Who should they call, where should they go, and what should they do? Consider posting information, emergency contact names, and phone numbers in an easy-to-access location.

- *Teach your child how to use 9-1-1.* A child needs to know when to call, for what reason, and the information that will need to be communicated so help can be provided.

- *Train older children in CPR and the Heimlich maneuver,* especially if they will be left at home with younger siblings.

- *Teach your child to safely handle and shoot a gun.* In the early teen years, we enroll our children in a hunter safety course so they learn safety and then we take them to a shooting range where they can gain confidence with a gun.

- *Provide basic self-defense measures.* Kidnapping, sex-trafficking, stalkers, muggings, active shooters, and robbery are all situations you should discuss with your child. The best defense is not putting oneself in a compromising situation. Talk about warning signs and wise actions to take if children find themselves in a dangerous situation.

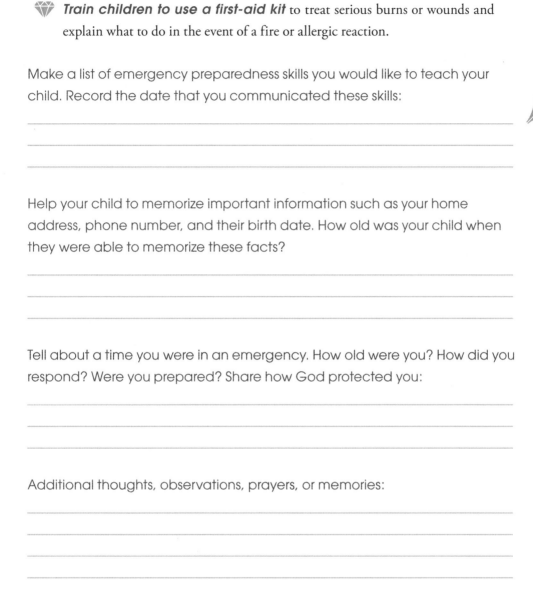

💎 ***Train children to use a first-aid kit*** to treat serious burns or wounds and explain what to do in the event of a fire or allergic reaction.

Make a list of emergency preparedness skills you would like to teach your child. Record the date that you communicated these skills:

_____

_____

_____

Help your child to memorize important information such as your home address, phone number, and their birth date. How old was your child when they were able to memorize these facts?

_____

_____

_____

Tell about a time you were in an emergency. How old were you? How did you respond? Were you prepared? Share how God protected you:

_____

_____

_____

Additional thoughts, observations, prayers, or memories:

_____

_____

_____

_____

_____

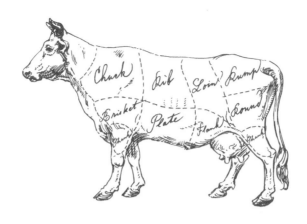

UNDERSTANDS NUTRITION
AND MAINTAINS A HEALTHY DIET

Our bodies are a gift from God, a reflection of His creation, and part of honoring God with our bodies is to take care of it. A healthy body gives us energy to work, play, worship, and serve God and those around us. The Bible reminds us "So, whether you eat or drink, or whatever you do, do all to the glory of God" (1 Cor. 10:31). Gluttony is a sin to avoid in Scripture yet an indulgence that is encouraged today in our society, so it is a major temptation that your child may need to conquer through Christ. It takes knowledge and discipline to maintain a healthy diet, and you are just the person to teach this to your child.

Teach your child the difference between real and processed foods. Real foods include very few ingredients, ideally fewer than five. Fresh fruit, vegetables, cheeses, meat products and nuts are all examples of real foods. Real foods tend to contain more water and fiber and less preservatives. Processed foods are those composed of multiple ingredients, often made in a factory setting. Processed foods generally contain more preservatives and sometimes artificial colors, flavors, and chemicals.

Offer real foods before processed foods. Infants, toddlers, and young children are developing their tastes and food preference. Give your child a head start on good eating patterns by introducing healthy foods when he or she is little. Fruits and vegetables are perfect for little hands and make excellent snacks. In our home, we keep a bowl of apples, oranges, and bananas on the counter, and bags of baby carrots, mini cucumbers and string cheese easily accessible in the refrigerator. These snacks are always available to be eaten without restraint, while we limit processed foods.

Help your child make wise food choices. Children (and adults!) will often gravitate toward eating sugary, starchy, and unhealthy foods when given the opportunity. Encourage your child to eat a balanced diet. Monitor portion sizes, but do not shame a child who eats heartily. In the same way, do not let food become an area of conflict; refrain from forcing your child to finish portions of foods they do not enjoy. Instead, encourage your child to take a few bites of a new food. Cook healthy recipes together that you all will enjoy.

Encourage your child to drink water. Sports drinks, sodas, and juices provide very little nutrition and many added calories to your child's diet. Water is good for your child's skin, hair, digestion, and overall health. If your child doesn't love the flavor of water, add a few fresh berries or drops of lemon. Consider purchasing a water bottle for your child that they can fill up and use throughout the day both at home and away.

Develop a biblical theology of food and eating. Study what the Bible has to say about food. Read passages together such as Genesis 1:29, Genesis 9:3, Ecclesiastes 9:7, and Matthew 6:25. To gain greater clarity for conversations with your children, consider reading books about how God's creation interacts with our modern food system in books such as *The Marvelous Pigness of Pigs* by Joel Salatin.

Warn young adults of the dangers of addictive substances that could master their lives and steer them away from Christ. Children need wise counsel about the addictive potential of highly caffeinated drinks, smoking, marijuana, and alcoholic beverages. Children need to know that drunkenness is a sin, that alcohol has ruined many lives, and that drinking carries with it immense danger. Alcohol consumption, smoking, and marijuana use are significant temptations for many teens, who need to be equipped how to say no and not place themselves in compromising situations.

Model healthy habits for your child. Despite learning about the food pyramid in school, I (Jen) didn't understand commonsense nutritional habits until I was in my late twenties, when I met a personal trainer and nutritionist who worked with me to prepare my body for pregnancy. I learned about how to eat a balanced diet of good food, not labeling foods "good or bad," and how to appreciate the body God gave me. Our children will see and learn from the messages we communicate to them in all areas of life, including how we view food.

How do you model a healthy diet and nutrition to your child:

_____

_____

_____

_____

_____

Describe some of your weekly favorite family dinner menus. Who typically does most of the cooking? Where do you sit for dinner? What dishes do you use? What do you drink:

_____

_____

_____

_____

_____

_____

Ask your child the following questions at age five, ten, and fifteen. Record their answers here.

What is your favorite thing to eat for breakfast?

Age 5: _____

Age 10: _____

Age 15: _____

If you were going to make a sandwich, what would you put on it?

Age 5: _____

Age 10: _____

Age 15: _____

What is your favorite fruit?

Age 5: _____

Age 10: _____

Age 15: _____

What is your favorite vegetable?

Age 5: _____

Age 10: _____

Age 15: _____

What is your favorite beverage?

Age 5: _____

Age 10: _____

Age 15: _____

What is something you like to eat for dinner?

Age 5: _____

Age 10: _____

Age 15: _____

What is your favorite kind of ice cream?

Age 5: _____

Age 10: _____

Age 15: _____

What is your all-time favorite dessert?

Age 5: _____

Age 10: _____

Age 15: _____

What is your favorite restaurant and what do you order there?

Age 5: _____

Age 10: _____

Age 15: _____

What food do you most enjoy for a special occasion?

Age 5: _____

Age 10: _____

Age 15: _____

If you could eat one food every day what would it be?

Age 5: _____

Age 10: _____

Age 15: _____

If you could eat a meal with any person, dead or living, who would it be?

Age 5: _____

Age 10: _____

Age 15: _____

Additional thoughts, observations, prayers, or memories:

_____

_____

_____

KNOWS HOW TO
DRESS APPROPRIATELY

G arth Brooks begins one of his songs, "Blame it all on my roots, I showed up in boots and ruined your black-tie affair." Apparently, Garth's parents didn't teach him how to dress appropriately, and he showed up for a formal event wearing casual clothes. Maybe you've heard the popular sayings "dress for success" and "dress for the job you want, not the job you have." Whether in songs or sayings, society recognizes that clothing choice matters.

The Bible has a lot to say about clothes. Clothing was given to Adam and Eve by God to cover their nakedness due to sin. The gift of clothing reminds us of a God who sees our sinful condition and covers us through the sacrificial death of Jesus. Physical clothes are a symbolic reminder that believers are clothed by the righteousness of Christ. The Bible emphasizes modesty, inner beauty over outer beauty, and dressing in accordance with one's sex. Children can be taught these principles and to think about their clothing choices by asking, "What am I trying to accomplish or communicate with the clothes I wear?"

My (Jen's) dad lightheartedly tells stories of being in sixth grade and his dad taking him shopping for school clothes. His dad, my grandpa, took him to Sears, walked into the boys clothing department and picked up five plaid button-down shirts and five pairs of navy pants. My grandpa then very practically said out loud, "Monday, Tuesday, Wednesday, Thursday, Friday." My dad also has stories about a boy who sat behind him in class and made charts keeping track of the fact that my dad wore the same red plaid shirt every Monday, blue on Tuesday, and green on Wednesday. My dad still wears plaid shirts with navy pants, calling them his "uniform," but he is meticulous with the patterns and styles, and is sensitive to criticism of his fashion choices.

Something as simple as clothing choices can carry tremendous impact for our children. Your child's clothing should be appropriate for the occasion, honor God, and fit well. Selecting the right clothing will instill confidence, create perceptions about them in others, and lead to a positive first impression. Help your child to dress appropriately by considering the following suggestions:

◆ *Help boys dress masculinely and girls dress femininely.* Help your daughter to dress like a woman and your son to dress like a man. Affirm your son when he wears a button-down shirt or your daughter when she puts on a dress. Require that your child dress according to their biological sex, as this reinforces God's good design of manhood and womanhood. The Bible recognizes distinctions between the sexes and warns against cross-dressing (Deut. 22:5).

◆ *Teach your child to choose clothing that is appropriate for the activity.* When your children are young, communicate what you would like them to wear for church, school, work, play, and special occasions. Provide the clothing to meet your expectations. For example, if you would like your daughter to wear a dress to church, provide her with two to three dresses along with tights and shoes that she enjoys wearing. Do not give young children the authority to choose their clothes or you may find yourself fighting clothes battles through the years.

◆ *Help your child to select clothing for special occasions in advance.* I have been performing in musical concerts and recitals for as long as I can remember. There's nothing more distracting or stressful than needing to perform in front of a room full of people in uncomfortable clothes or shoes. The same would be true of an athlete, scholar, or artist. Uncomfortable, distracting clothing should be avoided by advanced planning. When your child is little, you can do the advanced planning for them. As your child gets older, remind them of upcoming events and encourage them to begin the planning process themselves.

💎 *Discuss modesty and proper clothing fit with both boys and girls.* It is important to dress in a way that minimizes temptation for others. Help your child assess their clothes by asking a few questions. Are my clothes too big or too small? Am I able to move freely and comfortably? What is an acceptable length for shorts and skirts? Are the things I'm wearing reflective of my love for God and others? Because culture often sends negative messages to girls about fashion and body image, we recommend the book *8 Great Dates for Moms and Daughters: How to Talk about True Beauty, Cool Fashion . . . and Modesty!* by Dannah Gresh, as well as reading 1 Timothy 2:9–10 with your children.

💎 *Give guidance about appropriate swimwear.* Help boys and girls choose swimwear that fits well. Help your child evaluate if swimwear is prone to gaps or falling off. While we recognize that most swimwear is not modest, encourage modesty when your child is out of the water by teaching children to wear rash guards, T-shirts, or cover-up dresses.

💎 *Teach your child not to judge themselves or others based upon clothing.* The fashion industry does not define what is beautiful. God defines beauty, which has nothing to do with the clothes we wear (1 Pet. 3:3–4; Prov. 31:30). The Bible tells us in 1 Samuel 16:7 that "Man looks on the outward appearance, but the Lord looks on the heart." While everyone can see what is on the outside, only God can see what's on the inside. Choosing and wearing the right clothing is a valuable skill, but the development of one's inner character is most important.

What are your child's favorite pieces of clothing to wear? Describe them here.

0-5 years old:

_____

_____

6-10 years old:

_____

_____

11-14 years old:

_____

_____

15-18 years old:

_____

_____

Tell about a time your child wore something special for an occasion. What was the event? What did they wear? How old were they? How did they feel about wearing the outfit?

_____

_____

_____

Additional thoughts, observations, prayers, or memories:

_____

_____

_____

CHAPTER 16

EDUCATIONAL ESSENTIALS

TAUGHT TO READ AND
BE A LOVER OF GREAT BOOKS

Have you ever noticed that when you read a biography of somebody who was a pioneer, leader, or world-changer, they were often described as being somebody who loved to read? Books have the ability to teach us about God, ourselves, and the world around us. Great stories, like the ones about Frodo or Aslan, build the moral imagination, stir longings, and awaken us to truths in unexpected ways. Being a lover of great books not only engages the mind and imagination, but also gives children the ability to gain greater understanding of subject matter without the use of screens.

Throughout history, Christians have taught children to read so they can read the Bible on their own. Reading may be the single most important educational benchmark for a child, but of course there are many opinions about when and how to teach a child to read. Reading is a struggle for many children, in part because they are forced to read earlier than they are developmentally ready. When I (Josh) was taught to read, my experience was so negative that I only read a half dozen books on my own before graduating from high school, and it wasn't until later in life when I rediscovered the joy of reading. We have given our children space to read when they are ready, and it's been very successful. We've had children who were reading chapter books by age five and others who didn't begin reading until their grade-school years. But the common denominator for all of our children was an internal motivation to read that was cultivated by our children seeing us read as parents and reading aloud as a family. Every one of our children arrived at the point where they were practically begging us to teach them to read because they knew the treasures that awaited them in books.

In our home, reading great books out loud has become a favorite family activity. Beginning when our oldest son Jay was very young, I (Jen) would read to him so much that he would memorize the books in front of him. He knew the text so well that at the age of two, he would "read" *Pat the Bunny*, *The Big Picture Story Bible*, and *Goodnight Moon* out loud to me. Before we knew it, our second son, Asher, was doing the same thing. Gradually, as the children got older, we advanced to reading chapter books together in the evenings. We never read to our children with the intention of forcing them to love books. Instead, their love of books and reading stemmed from experiencing the richness of story and truth. We know our children love books because we catch them reading late into the night with a flashlight under their covers. Our children read so much that we had to make a rule that books are not allowed at meals. It's a normal day to find our children engrossed in a book. One of our fun family activities is to go to a thrift store or used bookstore to hunt for books. Today, all five of our children love to read and be read aloud to. We give our children books as gifts for each birthday and Christmas. They are excited to see what book they will receive next, and oftentimes toys will become second in line to be played with, only after they have explored the adventure awaiting them in a new book.

When teaching your child to be a lifelong learner and lover of great books, consider the following:

- *Whether your child is young or old, read to them out loud.* What a joy it is to experience the greatest books together! Books read aloud together shape your family culture, become the topic of conversation, and provide fantastic entertainment and endless discipleship opportunities. Don't waste your child's time and attention on twaddle. Snuggle up on the couch or hunker down for a road trip and read books that will enrich their imagination and shape their character. Our children's favorite books are the *Wingfeather Saga* by Andrew Peterson, the *Little House* books by Laura Ingalls Wilder, and books by Roald Dahl, J.R..R Tolkien, C.S. Lewis, and J.K. Rowling. If you need help selecting books, we recommend purchasing resources with hand-selected book titles, such as *Honey for a Child's Heart* by Gladys M. Hunt and *Books Children Love* by Elizabeth Laraway Wilson, or utilize book lists from Ambleside Online or Carole Joy Seid.

◈ **Purchase your child books they will love to read again and again.** What are their hobbies and interests? Who do they look up to? What kinds of stories are they drawn to? Give your child books that appeal to them and you will set a pattern of lifelong learning and reading. A book whose home is on your bookshelf will be revisited again and again.

◈ **Choose books that will shape your child's worldview.** Read *The Chronicles of Narnia* by C.S. Lewis and experience the greatness of Aslan, or *The Pilgrims Progress* by John Bunyan and reflect upon Christian's burdens. Children of all ages will be engaged and challenged by well-written works by Christian authors. Seek out colorfully illustrated editions of these books to further engage the imagination.

◈ **Read biographies of men and women from church history.** See the section on teaching church history on page 125.

◈ **Encourage books first, screens second.** The smell of ink, the texture of the paper, the grain of the cover, and the sound of pages turning—there is an aesthetic to reading an actual book that cannot be replicated on an electronic device. Whenever possible, we encourage our children to experience a physical copy of a book. It is very easy to type a word into an online search when needing to find a definition, but the act of looking a word up in a physical dictionary or thesaurus is one that teaches a myriad of skills. Instead of opening

Books, books they are like hooks that
always cling to me

They can take you anywhere, like down
the slopes on skis.

In books you can go to Hawaii, and
even Timbuktu

Most books are so very good that you
should read one too.

Jenny Mulvihill, age 8

up the internet to identify birds or plants on a nature walk, bring a field guide instead. The beauty of this method is the trail of learning that is created. By doing an online search for the name of a bird you will receive that information and be finished. In contrast, opening a field guide of birds will display many birds, perhaps from the same region. The same is true of walking the aisles of a bookstore or library. One book leads to another and then another, unlike the unilateral isolated information accessed online.

How old was your child when they learned to read? What was the first book they read on their own?

_____

_____

_____

Make a list of your child's favorite books. What made these books a favorite selection?

Ages 0-5:

_____

_____

_____

Ages 5-9:

_____

_____

_____

Ages 10-14:

_____

_____

_____

Ages 15–18:

_____

_____

_____

Describe the books you read out loud together and special memories made:

_____

_____

_____

What books did you give your child to help shape their worldview and faith in Jesus Christ? Record the titles and date given here:

_____

_____

_____

What were your favorite books when you were a child? Why were they your favorites? Who gave them to you? How old were you when you read them?

_____

_____

_____

Additional thoughts, observations, prayers, or memories:

_____

_____

_____

_____

APPRECIATES MUSIC AND HAS MUSICAL OPPORTUNITIES

Throughout the Bible we see music as an expression of our praise and worship of God. It is used to tell of God's great deeds, offers outlets for both lament and praise, and provides unity to God's people. An entire book of the Bible, Psalms, is devoted to music. Scripture is full of recorded songs. David, Moses, Hannah, Mary, and Zechariah are just a few examples of people in the Bible who used song to communicate their trust, faith, and love of God. The playing of instruments is highly spoken of in Scripture. Martin Luther noted the value of music when he stated, "Next to the Word of God, music deserves the highest praise. The gift of language combined with the gift of song was given to man that he should proclaim the Word of God through Music." [11]

While some people may view music as unnecessary, the Bible clearly sees it as an essential element of the Christian faith. Colossians 3:16 encourages us, "Let the word of Christ dwell in you richly, teaching and admonishing one another in all wisdom, singing psalms and hymns and spiritual songs, with thankfulness in your hearts to God." A deep appreciation and love of music, and the ability to make music is something to strive to teach each of our children.

Use music to memorize the Bible and teach theology. What is sung by song is remembered long. Music has the power to give permanency to memories. How many of us have a difficult time remembering important dates and facts, yet can sing every line of commercials from our childhoods as soon as the melody is played? This same lasting effective memory tool can be used to sing and memorize the Bible. Both Seeds Family Worship and Roots Kids Worship are excellent resources for helping your child learn core doctrines in a way that is both fun and memorable.

 Give your child the opportunity to learn a musical instrument or sing in a choir. The Bible gives instruction in Psalm 150:6: "Let everything that has breath praise the Lord!" Whether it be piano lessons, learning an instrument in the school band, or singing in the church choir, learning musical expression is a skill your child will use for their entire life and is a direct implementation of Psalm 150. Our children all learned to play musical instruments and sang in children's choirs during their elementary years. As their skills grew, hearing them make music together has brought our family tremendous joy. Their musical skills have given them the opportunity to bless others by singing and playing their instruments together for extended family gatherings, leading worship at church, and as an activity enjoyed together, and will allow them to incorporate music into their own homes as future adults.

 Make music a central theme. Throughout the year we choose music that is fun and fits the seasons. One fall we sang the soundtrack to the *Sound of Music* so many times even our two-year-old could sing the entire song, "How Do You Solve a Problem Like Maria?" We listen to oldies and the Beach Boys while fishing at the lake. Last Christmas we intentionally learned the themes in *The Nutcracker Suite.* One summer we learned "Oh What a Beautiful Morning" from Oklahoma to sing while taking walks down the gravel road and past the dairy farm next to our home. Each Easter we learn a new hymn, taking time to learn and sing the verses in the weeks leading up to Good Friday. Be creative and create your own soundtrack for your home.

Experience truly skilled musicians. Instill in your children a deep appreciation for music by seeing it and hearing it in person. It is good to support local community performances, and if possible, attend professional concerts, recitals, and Broadway plays. I will never forget hearing Isaac Stern perform Mendelssohn's Violin Concerto Op. 64, sitting in the fourth row for *Hamilton* on Broadway, taking in Andrew Peterson's Resurrection Letters tour, and hearing Handel's *Messiah* performed with all of its nuance and beauty. The musical skill and artistry on display in those settings would inspire anyone to attempt to belt out a tune or tune up their instrument.

Read the following Scripture passages with your child. Summarize below what they teach us about the role of music in our lives:

Psalm 104:33 _____

_____

Psalm 150 _____

_____

James 5:13 _____

_____

1 Chronicles 16:23–25 _____

_____

Ephesians 5:18–19 _____

_____

Make a list of the musical songs, styles, and artists you want your child to be familiar with:

_____

_____

_____

_____

_____

Describe your favorite family songs to sing together. When did you start singing them? How often do you sing together? Where do you sing:

_____

_____

_____

Tell about special memories made together experiencing music, concerts, and theatrical productions. Include as much detail as possible.

_____

_____

_____

Is your child learning to sing or play a musical instrument? Share how they chose their instrument. Who are they learning from? What were their first performance opportunities?

_____

_____

_____

Did you play a musical instrument as a child? If so, describe your instrument, experiences, and any memories you have:

_____

_____

_____

Additional thoughts, observations, prayers, or memories:

_____

_____

_____

PROFICIENT AT BASIC MATH

Whether you were a whiz at math or struggled to get a C in geometry, basic math skills are required for daily life and are something you can teach your child. Preparing food, balancing your budget, tackling home improvements, and even reading the gas gauge in your car require adding, subtracting, multiplying, and dividing numbers. Teaching basic math involves helping your child have the skills to succeed in math and applying them to their everyday life. Teaching your child to become proficient at basic math does not mean you need to sit down with them and work through a curriculum. You won't break into a sweat trying to explain exponents and algorithms. Instead, encourage them to become comfortable using numbers to make their life easier.

Teaching your child proficiency in math is pointing your child toward Christ and the orderliness of His perfect design. Colossians 1:17 states, "He is before all things, and in Him all things hold together." Math is concrete and systematic. Numbers can be added, subtracted, multiplied and divided in succinct patterns with predictable outcomes. Perfection and order are a result of God's design. Math illustrates that God has a plan and that He is sovereign.

The little years:

💎 *Count everything!* Make the connection between numbers and amounts by counting toys, cereal, cars on the drive to church, ants on the sidewalk, anything!

Before you know it your little one will be asking, "What comes next?" and you will be counting to 100.

♦ *Have fun practicing basic addition and subtraction.* Give your child ten chocolate chips. Separate them into two piles. How many are in each pile? How many are there total? How many are left if you eat two? How many are left if you eat two more? If you are creative, this kind of activity can be replicated in many ways.

♦ *Give your child a tape measure.* When our son Jon was little, he loved to clip a tape measure to his belt and measure things everywhere we went.

The elementary years:

♦ *Play games!* Yahtzee, Uno, Chutes and Ladders, and Monopoly are all games that reinforce number skills.

♦ *Reinforce basic math concepts in lighthearted, creative ways.* Key concepts are addition, subtraction, multiplication, and division. Skip count by twos, fives and tens while driving to and from activities. Ask your child to try to stump you with addition or subtraction problems. Make up funny word problems.

♦ *Identify and count money.* Count coins and cash. Collect change in a jar and ask your child to count it. Divide coins into $1 piles.

♦ *Identify prices when shopping.* There are many, many math lessons to be learned at the grocery store. Allow your child to participate in weighing, counting, and figuring price per unit versus price per pound. Ask your child to read prices out loud for you. Task your child with comparing brands to find the best deal or keep a running list of the total amount of money needed to purchase the items in your grocery cart.

💎 **Have fun with fractions in the kitchen.** Bake a pie and measure the ingredients, using both liquid and dry measuring cups. Cut the pie into halves, quarters, and eighths to illustrate fractions. Experient with doubling and halving recipes to cook larger and smaller quantities of food as needed.

💎 **Plan purchases and spend their own money.** When your child has acquired money either as a gift or as a result of working, encourage your child to use cash. If your child desires to spend their money, plan the purchase in advance. Our daughter saved enough money to purchase a camera. Prior to visiting the store, we researched the best price online, calculated the amount of tax that would be collected, and brought the amount of cash. Our daughter counted out the cash and change due.

Junior high and high school:

💎 **Put their math skills to the test.** Assign your child tasks that involve household math, such as cooking, baking, sewing, or measuring. During our home renovation we added a tile backsplash in our kitchen. We asked our twelve-year-old son to record the measurements and calculate the square footage to be communicated to our general contractor. His measurements were accurate, and we had plenty of tile ordered for the project.

💎 **Open a checking or savings account.** Managing their own checking or savings account is excellent preparation for eventually managing a household budget. Regularly monitor the account with your child and discuss planned expenses.

💎 **Let them do the shopping.** Once your child is old enough to drive, task them with handling facets of household shopping. Provide your child with cash and a list of items to be purchased.

Assist with filing taxes. Students in high school often have part-time jobs that require the payment of income taxes. When this occurs for your child, sit down together and fill out the forms. Oftentimes, online calculators will make the calculations for you, but showing your child the percentage of their salary that is withheld for state and federal taxes will help them plan in the future and understand the inner workings of their paychecks.

What were fun memories of counting together during the little years?
Did you count unique or creative things?

_____

_____

_____

We enjoyed learning about fractions in the kitchen while preparing the following foods:

_____

_____

_____

Tell about a time your child used their math skills to help your family:

_____

_____

_____

Additional thoughts, observations, prayers, or memories:

_____

_____

_____

ENCOURAGED TO EXPLORE ARTISTIC OPPORTUNITIES

Our God is a creative God. Had He chosen, He could have created the world without color, texture, or variation. But He did not. He gave us a world filled with vibrant colors, textures, shades of light, patterns, and shapes. In turn, God has gifted us with the innate desire to create and experience beautiful art. Francis Schaeffer noted, "The lordship of Christ should include an interest in the arts,"[12] and the raising of a child to adulthood should as well. Art helps children appreciate truth, beauty, and goodness in a wide variety of forms such as dance, drama, painting, drawing, sculpture, literature, music, architecture, photography, theatre, and interior design.

In Exodus 31, God instructs Moses to create the tent for the ark of the covenant. He mentions several artists whom He filled "with the Spirit of God, with ability and intelligence, with knowledge and all craftsmanship, to devise artistic designs, to work in gold, silver and bronze, in cutting stones for setting, and in carving wood to work in every craft." We see that God desires for His children to create and appreciate beautiful art, and in doing so we are ultimately teaching our children to glorify Him.

Ideas to teach your child to appreciate art:

Give your child the opportunity to create. Little ones can color or draw, put stickers on a page, experiment with glue and glitter. Allow older children to use varying items such as paint, pastels, clay, wood, photography, and textiles. If you are able, consider taking an art class together to learn new techniques.

Acknowledge the source of true beauty. C.S. Lewis said, "We do not want merely to see beauty, though, God knows, even that is bounty enough. We want something else which can hardly be put into words—to be united with the beauty we see, to pass into it, to receive it into ourselves, to bathe in it, to become part of it."[13] Beautiful art is only truly beautiful when it reflects God and His creation. The joy that we experience when we are pleased by something beautiful is a glimpse of heaven, and a taste of God's abundant love for us.

Experience original art. Visit an art gallery or sculpture garden. Purchase artwork for your walls or stone dinnerware from local artisans. Observe the details or brush strokes, color variant, scale, and texture.

Read books about art and artists. *Art and the Bible* and *How Should We Then Live?* by Francis Schaeffer are both rich theological texts exploring the relationship between art and worldview. Both would be appropriate for teenagers. For younger children, we have enjoyed beautifully illustrated books by Laurence Anholt, which tell the stories of famous artists including Matisse, van Gogh, Monet, Picasso and Degas. Purchase large coffee-table books of famous architecture, photography, or paintings and keep them within reach for your child to explore.

What are your child's favorite colors?

_____

_____

_____

_____

Ask your child to use their artistic skills to sketch and color a picture of your home from the outside when they are a toddler, in elementary school, middle school, and high school. Keep their drawings on the following page.

Describe the ways you see God has gifted your child with artistic skills:

_____
_____
_____

Tell about the art galleries, shows, and exhibits you visited. Where did you go? What artists did you see? What were your child's favorite works?

_____
_____
_____

Additional thoughts, observations, prayers, or memories:

_____
_____
_____

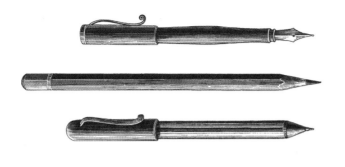

LEARNED HOW TO WRITE WELL

The ability to write well is a skill your child will need in their everyday lives as adults. To write is to give words to one's thoughts and to clearly share an idea or affection. Whether writing a letter to a grandparent, an assignment for school, an email for work, or writing creatively for pleasure, this skill is critical. Writing is about telling the truth, helping people see things anew, and learning about oneself and the world. Ants and orangutans do not share these yearnings, which is one reason they don't write. Writing is modeled by God, which displays its immense value. God's primary means of communication with us is through the written Word, the Bible. He has given us writing as a gift to be cultivated. We have stories to tell and a longing to communicate with others—to know and be known. The child who learns to write well has a skill that will enhance every job and every relationship, everywhere they go.

In the day and age of social media that emphasizes soundbites and visual images, writing well is not something that comes naturally to many young people. Good writing is a skill learned through practice, like using a scalpel or dancing the jig. Writing helps children learn critical thinking, how to persuade others, sentence structure, and good grammar. Becoming a good writer will help a child become a good reader and a good speaker. The child who can write well, read well, and speak well is one who can go anywhere and do just about anything.

💎 ***Give your child the tools they need to write.*** Begin with a notebook and a variety of pens and pencils. Do not offer constraints, only the space and time to freely write what comes to their mind. Once your child is able to write independently, resist the urge to constantly correct spelling, handwriting, and grammar.

💎 ***Learn to write legibly and to type.*** Poor penmanship is a speech impediment on paper. Work with a child to increase readability and legibility of their writing. Older children should learn to type.

💎 ***Read more.*** Reading helps children expand their vocabulary, see varying uses of language, methods of storytelling, or informative writing, and see grammar rules in action. It also helps them develop an understanding of how to share information in a clear, coherent, succinct way in nonfiction. Give your child access to a variety of literary genres including poetry, prose, fiction, nonfiction, research, jokes, and devotionals. Read from each of these genres and encourage your child to attempt to replicate the genre in writing.

💎 ***Make personal connections with writers.*** Visit local book signings to meet authors in your area. If your child has a favorite author, connect with them online. The Read Aloud Revival highlights beloved authors of children's literature and will host live Q&A sessions and author interviews.

💎 ***Learn how to write from great writers.*** Older children who want to learn about writing should consider reading *Adorning the Dark* by Andrew Peterson, *Bird by Bird* by Anne Lamott, *On Writing* by Stephen King, *Writing Tools* by Roy Peter Clark, and *Eats, Shoots & Leaves* by Lynne Truss.

💎 ***Give your child a reason to write by keeping a journal together.*** When getting started, it's helpful to have a focus for journaling. Children may enjoy keeping a prayer journal, nature journal, gratitude journal, or travel record.

Utilize creative writing prompts, such as *Tell Me a Story* by Jan McGrath, as a great way to foster journaling in older children.

Describe the ways you encourage your child to write creatively. What tools or supplies did you provide them with? Does your child enjoy the creative writing process?

_____

_____

_____

_____

_____

_____

_____

Ask your child to write out their favorite Bible verse in their very best handwriting. Save a copy here.

Write a letter to or a poem for your child:

_____
_____
_____
_____
_____
_____
_____
_____
_____
_____
_____
_____
_____
_____
_____
_____
_____
_____
_____
_____

Additional thoughts, observations, prayers, or memories:

_____

_____

_____

_____

_____

_____

_____

_____

_____

_____

CHAPTER 17

A DO-IT-YOURSELF PARENTING RETREAT

W̲e have been doing a DIY parenting retreat for almost two decades. These getaways have taken different formats over the years, but they have been a yearly practice that has aided our parenting efforts by helping us to arrive at a shared vision to raise children, to honestly assess where we were at with each child, and to identify key areas of focus for the next season of parenting. It was on a DIY weekend retreat that we created the list of items you saw earlier in this book, which has been fine-tuned as our children have grown and as we have matured as parents. The yearly rhythm of getting away to discuss, pray, play, and plan has been valuable for us, and we believe it will be helpful for you to get your bearings, evaluate how you are doing as a parent, and plan for the next portion of the journey.

Three Reasons You Should Go on a DIY Parenting Retreat

A parenting retreat is valuable because it

◆ Creates the opportunity to talk about your parenting. Most of us talk about our children plenty, but rarely is that discussion in-depth due to the pace of life and the presence of children. Our discussion often centers around daily schedules, behavior challenges, school or activity needs, or problem solving. A parenting retreat allows us to hit the parenting pause button, get away from the tyranny of the urgent, and get an accurate measure of how things are going.

💎 Encourages you to set aside a focused period of time to think about parenting priorities and plans. This section will help you evaluate how you are doing as a parent and develop a plan for the next season of parenting. It's a parenting check-in to help you step back, survey the big picture, and be more intentional in raising a child.

💎 Allows you to take a break from your children and, if you are married, have fun with your husband or wife! Parenting can be exhausting and all-consuming, so it is good and healthy to recharge and reconnect with your spouse. Not only that, but we are better parents when we are rested and relaxed.

Customize Your Own DIY retreat

DIY retreats can come in many different formats, so feel free to customize it to fit your needs and budget. When our children were younger and we had family who could watch our kids, Jen and I would get away to a hotel for the weekend. After both of our mothers died, it became more difficult to get away for the weekend, especially with five young children, because we had fewer people to watch our children. There were many years that we had to settle for a day trip or a series of evening dates. Over time, the Lord blessed us with the Westerberg family from our church, who offered to take our children once a year so Jen and I could get away, and that was one of the biggest blessings for us as a couple! Now that our children are older and more independent, it is easier to sneak away for larger chunks of time. Here are the three formats we utilized over the years:

💎 Plan a weekend getaway. Ask family or friends to watch your children for the weekend. Ideally, stay at a hotel so that you get away from the distractions of home and limit your drive to a few hours so that you don't spend too much time in the car. Build in time to talk, pray, have fun, rest, and plan.

◈ Set aside a full day and hire a babysitter so you can get away. Plan to go to a couple different places that day within a drivable distance of your home, to create some variety.

◈ An extended dinner at a restaurant or series of evening conversations at home. For some couples or single parents, a weekend getaway or even a day away isn't possible. Spread out the discussion over a series of dates during a month.

To begin, choose the format that works for you—a weekend, day trip, or evening get away. Put it on the calendar so that you block off the time and then begin to have fun planning the details! If you are a single parent, consider inviting a friend, a likeminded single parent, or your parent to join you for a daylong retreat. Allow time for solitary reflection on your parenting plan, but also include time to pray together, share ideas and resources, and have fun and fellowship.

Practical Tips for Your Time Away

Tip 1: Ideally, find a location other than your home. Our homes are filled with distractions—the dishes are piled high, the lawn needs attention, and it can be hard to focus on a parenting discussion when we are staring at these kinds of family and home management items. Jen and I have found that it can be hard to feel emotionally excited about a planning day or weekend when the house is a mess or there are ongoing projects that need attention. We've discovered it is best to get out of the house and away from the regular demands of our home and family. This may not always be possible due to circumstances, so if that is the case, do the best with what you have!

Tip 2: If you are stuck on a subject or an individual question, take a break or make a note and return to it in the future. If a disagreement arises and you cannot resolve the issue together, take time to pray together about the topic, and if the disagreement continues, then seek out a godly couple or a pastor from your church for counsel.

Tip 3: Make a commitment that there will be no insulting or attacking one another. If you are frustrated about something, make note of this in your mind, ask God to give you grace, and bring up the topic in a loving, respectful, and helpful way. Utilize the phrase "I feel" rather than "You did this," as it will generally lead to a more positive conversation. Remember, you are on the same team, so set down your weapons and love one another well! Don't spoil the getaway with a sarcastic, mean-spirited, or irresponsible comment that wounds the other person. Rather, seek to build one another up through encouragement, edification, and praise. We are all imperfect parents doing our best, so extend the same amount of grace to one another that Christ has extended to you.

Tip 4: Designate some time to pray with one another and for your children. Prayer lowers tensions, unites a couple, and centers our attention on God. Prayer is an admission that we are dependent upon God and invite Him into our time and conversations. Prayer makes a difference, so make sure to include it in your getaway.

Tip 5: Spend your personal devotion time leading up to the getaway, or devote time on your retreat, to reading some parenting texts in Scripture. The Bible is the all-sufficient authority on parenting, and we want it to guide our thinking and decision-making. Suggested texts include Deuteronomy 6:1–9; Psalm 127; Psalm 78:1–8; Proverbs 1–10; Ephesians 6:1–4; Colossians 3:20–21; 2 Timothy 1:3–7; and 2 Timothy 3:14–17.

Tip 6: Balance talk time with fun. A good getaway includes time to enjoy being with one another, or to have fun as a single individual, and time to discuss parenting. Jen and I often chose a location that had a wood fireplace, so that we could cozy up together in front of the fire while we discussed parenting topics. We would also choose a location that had activities for us to do together. We have great memories of learning to cross-country ski on a weekend parenting retreat, ice skating, boating, hiking, playing Yahtzee or cribbage, shopping together, and even playing bingo and ping-pong! One year we did a coffeehouse crawl and went to three or four different coffeeshops during the course of a day.

Tip 7: Create space to rest, if needed. In our early years of parenting, we would often need to catch up on sleep, so we planned a more relaxed schedule. It's amazing how much better life is with sleep!

Tip 8: Write down what you talk about so that you have a record for the future. We made the mistake of being unorganized early in our getaways. We did not have a central place where we recorded our discussion items. As a result, we would regularly search for notes or try to remember what we talked about. We created built-in places in this book to help you do this well.

Tip 9: Go through the questions and identify which ones you would like to cover during your getaway. Not every question is helpful for every home, so mark the ones you think will be the most helpful for you. Prioritize the most important questions first to ensure that you cover them, and if you have time, add some of the others that would be nice to include. Jen and I often found we were more ambitious than was realistic.

Getting Started

To help you, we've provided a list of questions that can be used to generate discussion or guide thinking about parenting. We want to assist you in getting a snapshot of where you're at and help you gain a clear picture of where you need to go. Our hope is to get you talking, thinking, praying, and planning about your parenting.

The questions uncover assumptions that might otherwise lurk as invisible landmines or unexpected blind spots. The questions provide the opportunity to help you do the work of parenting as well as work on your parenting. Both are needed. They will also help you clarify what matters most as parents!

QUESTIONS

Writing Your Plan

After reading through the 50 topics outlined earlier in this book, begin by making a plan for your child(ren) for the coming year. Repeat this process each year.

◆ Which of the 50 Things would you like to teach your child in the coming year? Aim to choose at least one, but consider multiple items to focus on during the next twelve months. Write down which of the 50 Things you will focus on for each child.

What are your goals or objectives for your child over the next six months, three months, and one month? Break your yearlong plan into tangible goals.

What specific resources and books do you plan to use to train your child in these areas? Where will you acquire them? List the resources you plan to use. If possible, order them during your planning time.

What hands-on activities or events will you utilize? Plan specific dates for these activities or events. Add those dates to your family calendar.

Who can assist you in the coming year? How can you include grandparents or extended family, close friends, a small group, or a creative gathering to accomplish one of your 50 Things? During your planning time either communicate your idea to these individuals and invite them to participate in a specific way or contact them and schedule a time to talk in the future about how they may contribute.

Set aside a date to assess your goals mid-year. This could be a discussion over coffee or an evening out. If possible, add a specific date or reminder on your calendar.

When you accomplish one of your 50 Things, capture the memories and milestones in writing at the end of that section along with any details, pictures, or items that would be special for your child.

Remembering the Past Year

◆ What successes and challenges did you experience as a parent this past year? What are some parenting high points and low points?

◆ Reflect on the ways each child has grown or matured in the past year. What fruit is being displayed? What skills have been learned? What character traits have been manifested regularly?

◆ On a scale of one to ten, how would you rate yourself as a parent this past year? What would it take to increase one or two numbers this year?

_____

_____

_____

_____

_____

_____

_____

_____

Parenting Role

◆ How do you feel about your parenting role? Your spouse's role?

◆ For the husband: Have you shown godly leadership for your home or have you abdicated this role? For the wife: Have you faithfully managed your home and been a godly helper to your husband?

◆ Have we prioritized our marriage over our children or are they coming between us as husband and wife in any way?

◈ What three things do you find most rewarding about parenting? What three are most frustrating?

◈ What challenges are you facing as a parent? What joys are you experiencing?

◈ Name one godly attribute or one parenting skill you would like to improve on this year. Is there any way your spouse can help you pursue this goal?

◈ How are you doing emotionally? Spiritually? Physically? Relationally?

◈ What have you been thinking about or worrying about as a parent?

◈ How do you feel about your responsibilities as a parent: overwhelmed and frustrated, content and organized, or something different?

◈ What things do you appreciate that your spouse does for or with the children?

◈ Name one way your spouse can serve or support you that would be helpful in our parenting?

◈ Is there anything your spouse could do that would make you feel more loved?

Parenting Goals

💎 Think back to your childhood. What were your parents' goals for you?

💎 What are your parenting goals? What qualities do you want to see developed in your children? By the time they are 21, what type of person do you want them to be? What do you want them to be prepared to do?

💎 Compare your goals with the goals that God has for parents in the Bible. Study the following verses to understand what God wants His children to become: Matt. 28:19–20; Ex. 20:1–17; Matt. 22:36–40; Eph. 4:1–6:20; Rom. 12:1–15; 1 Cor. 13; Phil. 2:1–18; 4:1–9; Matt. 5:1–7:27; Luke 6:27–49; Gal. 5:13–6:10.

💎 Discuss how you will raise your children to become what God wants each child to become. Study 2 Tim. 1:5; 3:15–17; Deut. 6:4–9; Heb. 12:5–11; Prov. 3:11–12; 1:8–9; 22:6, 15; 24–25; 13:20, 24; 29:15; Eph. 6:4; 1 Tim. 4:16; 5:8; 1 Cor. 15:33; Gal. 6:7–8.

💎 Study Deut. 6:4–9; Eph. 6:4; Prov. 1:8–9.

- What are the parental responsibilities mentioned in these passages?
- Discuss how you are currently doing implementing the responsibilities mentioned in these passages.

💎 According to Scripture, how would you summarize and personalize God's mission for your family?

💎 Examine the kind of discipline you provide your children. Discuss the following questions:

- What are your disciplinary rules? Are you clear in what you expect? Do your children understand the rules? Are you consistent with what will happen if a rule is not followed?
- Do you administer discipline consistently and fairly?
- Do you administer discipline in anger or under control?
- Do you administer discipline with love and instruction?
- Do you expect obedience immediately or allow a certain amount of disobedience?
- Do you both agree and support each other on the methods of discipline?

What are the most important character traits we want to see our children develop? Read and discuss Gal. 5:22–23; Col. 3:12–14; Phil. 2:3–4.

Examine what you are teaching your children about doctrine, apologetics, world-view, and cultural topics of the day.

_____

_____

_____

_____

_____

_____

Strengths and Affirmation of Children

Name one thing about each child that brings you great joy.

List each child by name and write down three to five things you appreciate about each child. Continue adding to the list as things come to mind. Communicate the items on this list to your child.

◈ Make a list of at least five fun things each child enjoys that you can do with him or her. Schedule a time in the next month to do at least one of these fun things with each child individually.

◈ List each child by name and write down his or her areas of strength and ways you could help each child continue to grow.

_____

_____

_____

_____

_____

_____

_____

_____

_____

Communication

In general, how are we doing in our communication with one another? When was the last time we had an in-depth conversation about how our children are doing spiritually?

◈ Have you been quick to listen and slow to speak (Jas. 1:19)?

◈ Have you regularly given godly encouragement (Eph. 4:29) and godly admonition (Prov. 24:26)?

◈ Do you use a gentle and loving tone when you speak to your children (Prov. 15:1)?

◈ Are you quick to forgive your children (Eph. 4:32; Isa. 43:25)? When was the last time you said "I'm sorry" or "please forgive me"?

◈ When was the last time you asked each child, "How are you doing?"

◆ Have you developed any communication habits that are negative or hurtful?

◆ Do you ever tend to speak harshly, scold, put down, or blow up at your children?

◆ Do you ever not listen to them or give them the silent treatment?

◆ Are there any ways you can improve your communication?

How would you describe the quality and frequency of communication with each child?

◆ What has helped you communicate well with any of the children?

◆ What hinders communication with any of them?

◆ Is there any child who is difficult to communicate with?

◆ What can you do to eliminate any communication barriers?

◆ What can you do to improve communication with the children?

Spiritual Climate of the Home

◈ How are you doing with family worship/devotions? Do you need to do anything to change or improve your time in God's Word as a family?

◈ What items or topics should you commit to praying about for your children? Make a list of topics that are important to you. Choose a theme verse to pray for each child and an individual verse for each prayer item.

◈ What biblical truths have you taught your children in the past year? What key biblical truths do you want to teach this year?

_____

_____

_____

_____

_____

_____

_____

_____

_____

Relationship with Children

◈ How would you describe your relationship with each child?

◈ What has helped you develop a good relationship?

◈ Has anything hindered you from developing a better relationship?

◈ What could be done to improve your relationship?

◈ Are there any unresolved problems, hurts, or sins that need to be addressed with a child?

◈ When was the last time you told each child "I love you"? When was the last time you hugged each child?

◈ Is our emotional intimacy with each child strong or weak? If it is strong, what needs to be done to maintain this connection? If it is weak, what needs to be done to strengthen it?

◈ Put yourself in the place of your children and imagine what you would want from a parent if you were in their shoes. What would you wish from a parent? What kind of home would you desire? What kinds of investments and attitudes would you appreciate from a parent? Make a list of items without compromising biblical principles.

◈ List at least five ways you can show love to your children. Consider their hobbies and the things they like doing. Pick one item and plan a date in the next month with each child.

◈ Is your home an inviting place for your children's friends?

◈ Are your children showing wisdom in their choice of friends?

Family Health and Schedule

◆ Are you happy with your current work and family life balance? Are there any adjustments that need to be made?

◆ What activities or commitments are prioritized on your family calendar? What does this reveal about your goals for your children?

◆ Are you happy with your current family life and activity balance? Are your children benefiting from extracurricular activities? Are these activities too costly financially or spiritually, or impacting your family time together? Do your children have too many activities?

◆ Are there any outings or vacations you want to take as a family this year? When and where?

◆ What is each of our children struggling with? How can you shepherd them through these struggles?

_____

_____

_____

_____

_____

_____

_____

_____

_____

_____

_____

_____

Extended Family

◆ How is your relationship with grandparents? Siblings? In-laws?

◆ Are you communicating regularly with grandparents and including them in your family life?

◆ Are there any new or additional ways grandparents could engage spiritually with your children?

◆ Are you planning any trips or time to see extended family this year?

◆ How can you be an encouragement to your extended family this year?

_____

_____

_____

_____

_____

_____

_____

_____

_____

_____

How have you been doing in the following areas as parents:

◆ I become angry and lose my temper. (What do you get angry about? Note what occasions cause you to lose your temper.)

◆ I nag or criticize the children. (What do you nag them about?)

◈ I am irritable and can sometimes be difficult to be around.

◈ I am anxious and often worry about the children. (What do you worry about?)

◈ I can be harsh or sometimes yell at the children. (Note what occasions cause you to be harsh or yell.)

◈ I complain about parenting tasks. (What tasks?)

◈ I keep a record of wrongs the children have done rather than forgive them.

◈ I am more concerned about godly character and Christian values than I am about performance, athletic skills, grades, or external beauty.

◈ I am sensitive to the needs, fears, feelings, and opinions of each child.

◈ I am too lenient with children and allow them to get away with things they shouldn't.

◈ I make promises or threats to the children I don't keep.

◈ I give children the freedom to make decisions when serious issues are not at stake.

◈ I do not mock a child, make fun of him, belittle her in front of others or call the child dumb or stupid.

◈ I speak to the children in a loving, gentle, and patient manner.

◈ When I make a mistake, I admit it and ask a child for forgiveness.

◈ I do not expect perfection from a child.

◈ I place the needs of my spouse before children.

◈ I agree with rather than argue with one another in front of the children.

◈ I am consistent in when, why, and how I discipline each child.

◈ I prioritize work, ministry, or hobbies over parenting.

◈ I have created an environment where each child can approach me with fears, problems, or difficulties.

◈ I spend quantity and quality time with each child.

◈ I know each child's heart, thoughts, dreams, likes, dislikes, and fears.

◈ I am appropriately affectionate toward each child in word and action.

◈ I maintain the daily practice of praying for my children and with my children.

◈ I maintain the daily practice of reading and discussing the Bible with my children.

Church Involvement

◆ Have you prioritized weekly corporate worship at a Bible-preaching church? If you do not attend church regularly, what changes need to be made so that your family is more consistent in attendance?

◆ How do you feel about the family's level of involvement and relationships at your church?

◆ What ministries did your children participate in this year? If your children are not involved in church, what are some goals you have for this coming year?

◆ How is your family doing serving regularly in some capacity? Do you need to do anything to change or improve so that your family is more consistent in this area?

◆ Do you speak positively of the church and pastors in front of your children?

_____

_____

_____

_____

_____

_____

_____

On the next two pages, write out your family's mission statement based on the guidance found on pages 49 to 52.

OUR FAMILY
MISSION STATEMENT

Final Thoughts

Perhaps there are parenting concerns or questions that were not addressed in any of the previous categories. Is there anything else you should discuss?

_____

_____

_____

_____

_____

_____

_____

_____

_____

_____

_____

_____

_____

_____

_____

_____

_____

_____

_____

_____

_____

_____

_____

_____

ADDITIONAL MILESTONES AND MEMORIES

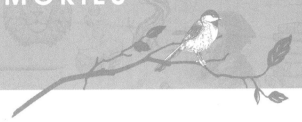

Print a favorite picture of your child as an infant, toddler, in elementary, middle and high school. Keep a copy here. Why are these your favorite photos?

Infant:

Toddler:

_____

Elementary:

_____

Middle school:

High school:

Share the story of how you chose your child's first and middle names. Why?

_____
_____
_____

What schools did your child attend for elementary, middle, and high school? How did you choose each school? Who were your child's favorite teachers? Share as many details as possible:

_____
_____
_____
_____
_____
_____
_____
_____

What is the school subject that comes naturally to your child? What is the most difficult, and how have you encouraged your child to enjoy both? List the activities, clubs, hobbies, or sports your child participated in. How long was your child a member of each group? How old were they? Record the names of your child's favorite coaches or mentors:

_____
_____
_____
_____
_____
_____
_____
_____
_____

Describe your family's primary vehicle. Was it a car, minivan, SUV, or other? Was it old or new? What color was it? Where did your child sit in the car? Share a fun memory of being in the car together:

_____

_____

_____

_____

Tell about a favorite vacation you took as a family. Where did you go? How did you get there? How old was your child? How long did you stay? Share a special memory of your time together:

_____

_____

_____

_____

Did your child ever experience a medical emergency or injury? Share the story of what happened:

_____

_____

_____

_____

_____

Does your child spend time with his or her grandparents? How often do they see one another? What do they enjoy doing together?

_____

_____

_____

_____

_____

Describe a major milestone in your child's life. How old was your child? What was the setting? Who was there? What made this moment important? Provide as much detail as possible.

_____
_____
_____
_____
_____

Describe the ways God has gifted your child with special talents and skills. In what ways does your child use his or her skills?

_____
_____
_____
_____
_____

What are your child's most wonderful character traits?

_____
_____
_____
_____
_____

Describe your child in ten words.

_____
_____
_____
_____
_____

Write a prayer for your child:

_____
_____
_____
_____
_____
_____
_____

What is some life wisdom you'd like to share with your child? Write it here.

_____
_____
_____

Tell some of your favorite memories with your child. One of my favorite memories together is:

_____
_____
_____
_____
_____

In what ways are you proud of your child? Record those ways here.

_____
_____
_____
_____

CONCLUSION

IMAGINE THE DAY

Imagine the day your child graduates from high school. You go to the graduation ceremony. You enter the auditorium and you can feel the energy, see the smiles and sense the anticipation. Everything quiets down as you hear the graduation processional, see the swishing robes, and watch the tassels bounce on graduation hats. You locate your child and remember the day you held that precious baby in your hands for the first time. You remember many special moments, such as when they lost their first tooth and when they learned to ride a bike. It was just yesterday they were climbing into your lap and asking you to read them a book. You remember the joy of watching them grow, discover their strengths, and develop their unique personality.

You look over at your spouse's face and notice a big smile. You also see a tear in the corner of one eye. You grab one another's hand and give a squeeze. Or perhaps you are experiencing this momentous occasion alone or with extended family. In either case, today represents an odd combination of emotions, immense joy for the many wonderful times and sadness that life will be different from this day forward.

Graduation is the end of an era and the beginning of a new chapter. For many parents, it marks a shift of authority structure, when a child is being launched into adulthood. This moment of life is the culmination of years of daily interactions, countless prayers, thoughtful planning, lots of hard work, and the grace of God!

You watch your child receive the diploma with pride. After the ceremony is over, your child finds you. With a big smile and a warm hug you are told, "I can't thank you enough for everything you did."

Imagine the day your child graduates. It may be a long way off or it may be right around the corner. Regardless, no one wants to arrive at this day wondering, "Did I do the right things?" "Did I teach my child what is needed for lifelong faith in Christ?" "Did I provide my child with the essential training and tools for adulthood?" We hope this book helps you answer all those questions with a confident YES!

And most important, we hope that God used the parenting investments you made to shape your child into a mature, godly adult who knows, loves, and serves Jesus.

ENDNOTES

1. J.C. Ryle, *Thoughts for Young Men* (Moscow: Charles Nolan Publishers, 2002), 12.

2. James Strock, *Theodore Roosevelt on Leadership: Executive Lessons from the Bully Pulpit* (New York: Crown Forum, 2003), 230–231.

3. John Paton, *Missionary to the New Hebrides* (Edinburgh: The Banner of Truth Trust, 1965), 25–26.

4. Thomas Chalmers, *The Expulsive Power of a New Affection* (Wheaton: Crossway, 2020), 36.

5. "Homeschooling Will Not Save Them," *Desiring God*, desiringgod.org, March 7, 2018, https://www.desiringgod.org/articles/homeschool-will-not-save-them.

6. "Smiling Is the Best Way to Make a First Impression," *Kelton News*, keltonglobal.com, February 26, 2013, https://www.keltonglobal.com/recognition/smiling-is-the-best-way-to-make-a-first-impression/.

7. C.S. Lewis, *The Collected Letters of C.S. Lewis Vol III: Narnia, Cambridge and Joy 1950–1963*, ed. Walter Hooper (New York: HarperCollins, 2007), 247.

8. Gene Edward Veith, *Here We Stand!: A Call From Confessing Evangelicals for a Modern Reformation*, ed. James Montgomery Boice (Minneapolis: Baker Publishing, 1996), 95.

9. C.S. Lewis, *Mere Christianity* (San Francisco: HarperOne, 2015), 77.

10. Emily Post, *Etiquette: Manners for Today,* 19th ed. (New York: William Morrow, 2017), 8.

11. Philip S. Watson, *Luther's Works*, vol. 33 (Minneapolis: Fortress Press, 1957), 323.

12. Francis Schaeffer, *Art and the Bible* (Downer's Grove: IVP Books, 2006), 18.

13. C.S. Lewis, *The Weight of Glory* (San Francisco: HarperOne, 2001), 43.